# Ask Me No Questions

## I'll Tell You No Lies

# ? ? ?

## How to Survive Being Interviewed, Interrogated, Questioned, Quizzed, Sweated, Grilled...

? ?

D1383162

## Jack Luger

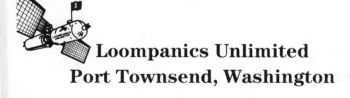

### Loompanics Unlimited
### Port Townsend, Washington

*This book is sold for information purposes only. Neither the author nor the publisher will be held accountable for the use or misuse of the information contained in this book.*

**ASK ME NO QUESTIONS, I'LL TELL YOU NO LIES: How to Survive Being Interviewed, Interrogated, Questioned, Quizzed, Sweated, Grilled...**
© 1991 by Jack Luger
Printed in USA

All rights reserved. No part of this book may be reproduced or stored in any form whatsoever without the prior written consent of the publisher. Reviews may quote brief passages without the written consent of the publisher as long as proper credit is given.

*Published by:*
Loompanics Unlimited
PO Box 1197
Port Townsend, WA 98368

Loompanics Unlimited is a Division of Loompanics Enterprises, Inc.

Cover design by Patrick Michael

**ISBN 1-55950-072-7**
**Library of Congress Catalog Card Number 91-061943**

# Contents

# Introduction

Life appears to be getting more complicated, and we have to cope with more pressure than our parents did. One of the types of pressure we face is the need to prevent or defend ourselves against people invading our privacy. In some cases, we have to answer questions from an interviewer or interrogator.

Many people face interrogation in one form or another during their lives. Sometimes it's during a criminal investigation. More often, an interrogation comes in a non-criminal setting, such as when applying for employment, or during a media interview.

There are techniques of obtaining information from willing and unwilling subjects, practiced each day by both skilled and unskilled interviewers. This book explains and lays out techniques of resistance, to help you avoid giving information or to conceal information while appearing to be cooperative.

In some cases, such as during a police investigation in the United States, you do not have to answer questions, because you're under the protection of the U.S. Constitution. However, police investigators have methods of inducing suspects to talk, despite Constitutional protection. You need to know about such techniques, which is why we'll examine these in detail.

In other situations, such as an employment interview, you're not under Constitutional protection. During employment interviews, you don't have to answer questions, but the employer doesn't have to hire you. In practical terms, that's coercion.

Your goal is to present a good picture of yourself, and conceal any derogatory information. If, for example, you once committed a crime and paid for your mistake in prison, there's no real need to reveal this to a prospective employer. Your honesty won't earn you any points, and you don't need to keep paying for your error for the rest of your life.

There are many reasons why the average person needs to defend himself. Perhaps the most important one is that the interrogator or interviewer is likely to be a pro, with much experience in his craft. He interviews people eight hours a day, forty hours a week, while most people face interviewers only occasionally. That gives the pro the edge.

Another reason is that interrogation and interviewing techniques have become very refined, and the average person needs a survival kit to protect himself. Techniques can be very subtle, designed to catch subjects off guard.

At times, you may not even know that you're being interrogated or interviewed. We'll examine how interviewers and interrogators use covert interrogations to capture damaging statements from unwilling subjects. Letting your guard down during such moments can lead to serious problems. Sometimes, an off-the-cuff statement can be construed as an admission of guilt, and people will later recall it and interpret it in the light of your presumed guilt.

Yet another reason is that many interrogators develop a cynical and distrustful mind-set, feeling that everybody lies. Even when faced with a truthful story, they'll be seeking gaps and inconsistencies. There are also investigators who feel pressured to find a likely suspect, and are willing to shade the truth in their eagerness to please the people paying their salaries. When facing one of these, it's almost a no-win situation.

People who need help in resisting interrogation mostly are not criminals. It's not a crime to apply for employment. It's also not a crime to be employed in a workplace where drug abuse or thefts take place. There are also people caught in circumstances they didn't create.

The wife of a real or suspected defector or spy, for example, may not know anything about his activities, but will come under intensive investigation. The relative of a criminal may also face suspicion. Friends, fellow employees, or associates of people suspected of crimes also come under a cloud, and need a survival kit to help them cope.

Certain political or social organizations often come under police or FBI investigation. These are the ones to which police assign labels such as "extremist." The currently fashionable term is "terrorist," applied to everyone from right-wing groups to environmentalists. An organization's actual actions are almost unimportant, because the stigma comes with the cause.

Sometimes, simply being there is enough. In cases of employee theft, company owners and managers suspect everybody, and may employ private investigators to ferret out the guilty parties. One individual found himself suspected when his employer mistakenly concluded that there was a stock shortage. In the end, it turned out that nothing was missing, and that the "shortage" had been a clerical error by the boss himself. However, this employee spent a couple of uncomfortable days under suspicion.

Another example is the employee whose firm hires undercover investigators to pose as employees to ferret out employee theft or drug abuse. To the undercover operative, everyone is a potential suspect, and genuinely innocent employees will come under his scrutiny. If you're in such a situation, you'll find out how uncomfortable it can be.

It's also possible to come under investigation for activities that are perfectly legal, such as labor union participation. Although the National Labor Relations Act forbids employers to investigate or punish employees for union activity, there's actually very lax enforcement of this prohibition. In real life, employers hire private investigators to work undercover and check up on employees' union activities.

Totally innocent people who lack self-confidence, and exhibit behavior that investigators interpret as deceptive, can be falsely suspected or accused. If you, for example, have trouble maintaining eye contact with the interrogator, you're in serious trouble, no matter how innocent you may be. If you answer in a hesitant manner, this can also provoke suspicion, to an interrogator trained in the linguistic school of thought. This is why average people need special training in conducting themselves credibly during interviews and interrogations.

Often, average people do fall under criminal investigation for unintentional infractions. One simple and common example is the drunk driver who runs over and kills a child. The police certainly will question him, if they know who he is. If not, they may have a list of likely suspects, and will work at narrowing that list.

The remorseful driver may be so overcome with guilt that he runs to the police to confess, or may break down into a tearful admission when an investigator knocks at his door. Admitting guilt won't bring the dead child back to life, and will probably harm the driver's family if he goes to prison. This is why we can make a good argument for resisting interrogation in criminal cases.

Society benefits from putting career criminals away for a long time. On the other hand, there's no benefit from ruthlessly imprisoning someone who is merely an accidental or situational offender. This can only ruin a career, tie up a prison cell and taxpayers' dollars that could see better use, and deprive the government of the taxes the person would be paying if employed.

American police officers are better than those in many countries, but they can still make mistakes. Although American officers do not willingly "frame" an innocent person just to get an arrest and clear a case, they can commit errors of judgment. In some cases, the evidence is ambiguous, and it's easy to draw the wrong conclusion. The Wylie-Hoffert murder case in New York, during the early 1960s, resulted in the police arresting the wrong man, at first, because they were under intense pressure to solve the case.

One question you might ask is whether this book will do more harm than good by falling into the wrong hands. The answer is, obviously, "no." The reason is that criminals already have this information. They know how to fool their interrogators, because they're street-smart and prison-hardened. In prison, which is really a crime university, they've taken the postgraduate course from more experienced offenders. In any event, many street criminals can't read. Organized crime figures also are adept at resisting interrogation. They have very clever attorneys, who practice deception every day, and coach their clients in the techniques.

We will cover physical torture briefly, because torture does take place in the United States, at times. We're not going to cover special situations, such as arrest by a foreign secret police, because most of you won't have to face such prospects. Nor will you have to endure drug interviews at the hands of CIA psychiatrists. The real hazards to average people come from average situations, such as employment and mistaken identity.

This book won't provide any magic formulas for beating interrogations. There are none. There are also no foolproof ways of extracting the truth from an unwilling or uncooperative subject. If you want to train yourself to resist interrogation, you'll have to work at it. You'll need to understand how different types of interrogations and interviews work, and memorize various tactics and countermoves. You'll have to rehearse some of your answers, and practice being interviewed. You'll have to practice before a mirror, to see yourself the way others see you.

This isn't back-breaking work, but you'll need to be serious about it. Some of it will be fun, as you see your skill improve. Most of all, the final results will be worth the effort.

# Part I:

# Tools And

# Techniques

# 1

# People Traps

There are several types of life situations that are traps, and people become caught in them for reasons not of their making. Some of these traps lead to interviews or interrogations.

Let's begin this study by laying out exactly what we mean by the word "trap." Obviously, a career criminal who burglarizes a house should not be very surprised if he's caught and questioned. On the other hand, someone riding in a vehicle with another person who gets stopped for a narcotics violation may be surprised, especially if he has nothing to do with the offense. It's guilt by association, one type of people trap, and falling victim to one of these traps is often merely bad luck.

There are different types. Let's look at a few hypothetical and real-life cases.

# Mistaken Identity

It's possible to be caught up in innocent ways. In a city with many people, it's almost inevitable that some people will resemble each other. A crime witness may provide police with a description that fits a dozen people, and if the description fits you, police will probably stop and question you.

# Police Entrapment

Police also conduct "undercover" and "pro-active" operations which sometimes roll up innocent people in the net. Some police officers go to cocktail lounges and other clubs to seek out narcotics violators. Youthful appearing undercover officers attend schools, enrolling as students. Undercover officers will even sell narcotics to arrest the buyers, according to U.S. District Judge Charles Hardy.[1] This borders on entrapment, but it happens because police are willing to skirt the edge of the law.

The problem with this sort of police work is that it tends to catch the little fish, the naive occasional or first offender, but not the hardened criminal who is street-smart and knows how to protect himself. If you, as a law-abiding citizen, attend a party during which someone brings illegal drugs, you may find yourself arrested as if you were the one who had instigated the affair. This can happen even without using drugs. Being there is enough.

# Carrying A Package

Some people are asked by friends or acquaintances to carry packages for them. This is usually an innocent request, but some people exploit their friends and acquaintances by asking them to carry illegal drugs and other contraband. If someone asks you to carry a package, especially aboard an aircraft or across a border, you should refuse unless you can see what's inside the package. However, if you trust that person, you might unwittingly end up ferrying contraband for him or her. This could happen even on a short trip across town, because some drug dealers use innocent friends to convey contraband past surveillance.

If you happen to be stopped while innocently carrying contraband, you may suffer confiscation of your vehicle, if it's in a state where the law provides for confiscation of any vehicle involved in drug trafficking. Police officers will almost certainly not accept any statement that you did not know what you were carrying. It's virtually certain that they'll interrogate you, but your answers may not help clear you.

## Physical Coercion

American police officers generally don't use physical violence against those they question, as the era of the "third degree" is long gone. However, police in some foreign countries do so as a matter of course. These foreign countries are not necessarily Iron Curtain countries, or "Third World" tyrannies. In Mexico, for example, it appears to be routine. The Sonoran Bar Association placed advertisements in Sonoran newspapers, on October 27, 1989, accusing police of torturing confessions from suspects to make them admit crimes of which they were innocent.[2] Surprisingly, the commander of the Sonoran Federal Judicial Police defended his officers by stating that they did not beat suspects in "bad faith."

An American arrested by Mexican police officers may expect the officers to read him his "rights," but "Miranda," although a

Hispanic name, does not apply South of the border. "Rights," as we understand them, do not exist. In many countries, in fact, it's an offense merely to refuse to answer a police officer's questions. In some, physical coercion, including severe torture, is legal.

## Emotional Isolation

When Edward Lee Howard, a former Central Intelligence Agency employee, defected to the Soviet Union, his wife Mary had to face questioning from the Federal Bureau of Investigation.[3] Although there's no evidence to suggest that Mary, herself a former CIA employee, had defected or passed any information to the Soviets, she had driven the car when her husband had eluded FBI surveillance and escaped.

On September 21, 1985, Howard prepared to ditch FBI surveillance by having his wife drive him on a circuitous course, so that he could jump out of the car immediately after rounding a curve. He'd prepared a dummy to place in the seat, so that pursuers seeing its silhouette would not become immediately aware that he'd escaped. Although his house was under watch, the FBI agent on duty somehow missed their departure, and for several hours, Howard and his wife were out of sight of the FBI. He arranged for his wife to play a tape recording of his voice on the telephone, to deceive listeners that he was still home. It wasn't until the following evening that Howard's employer notified the FBI that Howard had left him a letter of resignation.

The net result was that the FBI did not know that Mary had helped her husband escape. Although they may have suspected her help, for all they knew he had dropped out of a rear window and scurried down a gully, the same way John Dillinger had eluded them at Little Bohemia, Wisconsin, over half a century before. FBI agents did, however, question her. They were eager to find out if she had helped her husband in his espionage. There was some thought given to prosecuting her, but as they had no real evidence, they abandoned that idea.

At this point, Howard's wife had not actually broken the law. As Howard was not under arrest, he could not, by definition, be a fugitive. The FBI did, however, take advantage of her extreme emotional vulnerability to manipulate her. They brought in a sympathetic female agent to befriend her, and to help her cope with life without her husband. Mary, with a small son to raise, soon was cooperating, and went so far as to agree to a polygraph examination.

The FBI appeared to have milked her dry. She gave them information they could not have obtained any other way, such as the existence of a numbered Swiss bank account. She also revealed the location of a metal box containing about ten thousand dollars that Howard had buried in the desert, and went with agents who dug down and removed it. When they opened the box, they saw it contained bars of silver and assorted currency, including some South African Krugerrands.

This case is noteworthy because it shows how a single person can be made to feel isolated and vulnerable against the power of the state, and broken to the police's will, without physical torture or even severe threats. Although no detailed account of the interrogation sessions with Mary Howard are available, the main point is clear: the FBI had nothing against her, other than that she was a defector's wife. From that thin beginning, they extracted information from her by persistent and skillful interrogation, manipulating her emotions when she was most vulnerable.

Another case was that of Mike Rivera, wrongly convicted of a rape/murder in Philadelphia. According to an authoritative account of the case, police intimidated the main witness, as well as beat a confession out of the suspect.[4] The Rivera Case shows that, indeed, it "can happen here."

# Overzealous Security Staffs

At times, private security officers can suffer from excessive zeal, and try to coerce employees into admitting non-existent thefts. They may be working towards prosecution, in which case their object is to obtain a confession, or they may be seeking "restitution," in which case they try to obtain both a signed confession and money from the employee.

In one case that finished in federal court, an Eastern convenience store chain had employed security officers who coerced innocent employees into confessing to theft, under threat of prosecution, and had collected hundreds of thousands of dollars in "restitution." To date, over 300 former employees of the chain, Cumberland Farms, have become involved in a federal lawsuit against the firm, stating that they had been coerced into signing false confessions. The attorney handling the suit has estimated that the company may have coerced as many as 30,000 employees.[5]

One woman, who worked for the chain as a teen-ager, stated that her father had believed her guilty for 15 years. One divorced mother reported that when store security officers accused her of stealing $6,000, they threatened to take her children away from her, unless she handed over $1,500 in cash by noon on the following day. Another woman, who had admitted to taking unauthorized soft drinks while on duty, found security officers accusing her of having stolen $2,900.

Most or all of these cases appear to have started as interrogations, with security officers taking a suspect into a back room and insisting that they confess. These people allowed themselves to be victimized because they thought that they were alone, and that nobody, including relatives, would believe them. In that regard, they had some justification, because to some people, accusation equals guilt. Once some of the cases came to light, however, others who had been coerced into confessing began stepping forward, and some even formed a support group.

This shows the sinister side of private security. Although this is one of the few documented cases of abuse by private security officers, it illustrates the tip of the iceberg. There have been other instances of individuals falsely accused of shoplifting, for example, and coerced into signing confessions, but few have resulted in lawsuits against the abusers.

## Bad Luck

You don't have to be a criminal to fall under suspicion and investigation. Circumstances can cast suspicion on totally innocent people. If you're the unlucky one, you'll need all your wits about you in order to survive. You'll also need to know the basic facts about interrogation.

## Sources

1. Associated Press, November 17, 1989.

2. *Arizona Republic,* November 20, 1989.

3. *The Spy Who Got Away,* David Wise, NY, Avon Books, 1988, pp. 207-239.

4. *Notable Crime Investigations,* William Bryan Anderson, Editor, Springfield, IL, Charles C. Thomas, Publisher, 1987, pp. 315-321.

5. Associated Press, September 3, 1990.

# 2

# Interrogation:

# The Basic Facts

Let's begin by stating the obvious: an interview or interrogation takes place because the interviewer or interrogator needs information. If you, the reader, don't absorb anything else from this book, remember this one hard fact, because it's the foundation for everything else. In the following pages and chapters, we'll discuss many cases that highlight the same basic point.

The interrogator needs the information because he doesn't have it. He's questioning you because he hopes to get information from you. If you don't provide it, he may not be able to obtain it by other means. Sometimes, he has only part of the picture. He depends on you to fill in the rest, or to provide a lead to more information.

A skilled interviewer or interrogator's job is to persuade you to admit damaging information, or to incriminate yourself. An interviewer's manner is often bluff, to convince you that there's no point in withholding information. This works with many people, and they admit damaging facts about themselves when they could have successfully withheld them.

As a rule, people talk too much. This is true in employment interviews, criminal investigations, and various "internal" investigations that many employers conduct. In the majority of interviews, the main source of information, favorable or damaging, is the subject himself. Throughout this book, we'll be hitting at this point again and again, because it's vital. We'll discuss and study case after case in which people who could have avoided disclosing important information failed to protect themselves, and shot their mouths off to police and others. We'll also examine categories of information which are easiest to keep from interviewers.

## Interviews and Interrogations

Let's distinguish between an "interview" and an "interrogation." An interview is in a non-criminal setting, or at least with someone who is not under suspicion. The subject is usually willing to speak, because he's either witness to a crime, or because he has a positive reason for speaking, such as seeking employment. The subject also may be a neighbor, relative, or friend of a suspect, or have other information which can help an investigation.

An interrogation involves a suspect or co-conspirator who may have something to conceal. A superficially cooperative attitude may mask an intent to deceive.

There's often some overlap between the two categories because the distinction between witness, victim, and suspect isn't always clear during early stages of an investigation. An arson victim may have set the fire to collect insurance. A rape victim may be lying.[1]

This is why we'll often use the terms interchangeably. The tactics are often similar, and the objectives are the same. The interviewer/interrogator tries to elicit information, and the subject/suspect either tries to avoid giving it, or tries to put across his own version of the facts.

## Information vs. Evidence

In a criminal investigation, the officer who has all of the evidence he needs for a conviction doesn't need to speak with you. He's got his case, and he can convict you with absolutely no cooperation from you. If this is so, he won't be spending much time with you, but will simply throw your case into the lap of the prosecutor. This official will scrutinize the evidence, and form an opinion regarding whether or not he can easily win during a trial. Your attorney will make his own evaluation, and if he thinks he can't win an acquittal for you, will ask for an interview with the prosecutor. During this session, he'll explore the possibilities of working a deal. The prosecutor will decide how much the case is worth to him, in saving the expense and effort of a trial, and may make an offer which results in a "plea bargain." You plead "guilty" to a lesser charge, or to the same charge in return for a reduced sentence.

"Copping the plea" short-circuits the entire process. If you decide to plead guilty, the prosecutor doesn't have to present evidence, and he obtains a cheap win. Let's note here that, in reality, your actual guilt or innocence are almost irrelevant to the plea bargain. It's what the prosecutor can prove that counts, as well as your willingness to take or avoid the risk of a trial.

Most of the time, the interrogator needs a statement from you to use against you. The "Miranda" warning reads, in part: "Anything you say can be used against you in a court of law." In Great Britain, the "Judges' Rules" stipulate that the suspect receive the following warning: "Whatever you say will be taken down and may be used in evidence." This is less threatening than some fictional accounts in which British detectives warn the suspect that: "Everything you say will be used against you," but it's still enough to cause worry.

In many criminal cases, investigators don't have the physical evidence they need. Inducing the suspect to reveal where evidence is located helps assure a conviction. Many suspects don't realize how weak the investigators' case is, and they reveal details which only serve to make the case against them firmer.

## Understanding The Rules

Interviewers and interrogators often employ questionable tactics, systems, and devices, such as interpreting body language (kinesic interviewing) and using the polygraph, or "lie detector." The most important fact about these systems and devices is not whether they actually work or not, but that the interviewer thinks they do. Anyone undergoing interrogation of any sort must understand these systems, and act accordingly. Anyone who ignores them will risk being branded a liar.

## Do You Have to Talk?

Ernesto Miranda was a sleazy, small-time hood, arrested in Maricopa County, Arizona, in 1963 for rape and kidnaping. Miranda was not notable, in himself or in the nature of the charges against him, but his attorneys took his case to the U.S. Supreme Court, and the landmark decision that followed in

1966 bears his name. The Miranda Decision is based upon the Fifth Amendment, which protects against being forced into self-incrimination, and states that police officers must advise a suspect of his rights upon arrest, and before any interrogation. Supporting court decisions have broadened the meaning of the original ruling, so that officers cannot use information given voluntarily after an arrest but before they have read the suspect his rights.

For all that, Ernesto Miranda never changed his ways. He died from stab wounds received in a bar fight in 1976.

The Miranda Decision applies only to American police officers, but some other countries have similar safeguards for the accused. British and French police, for example, have to advise suspects of their rights, although in somewhat different language.

## The Miranda Warning

The result of the Supreme Court decision was the "Miranda Warning." The exact phrasing varies somewhat with the police agency, but the substance remains the same:

*You have the right to remain silent. If you give up this right, anything you say may be used against you in a court of law. You have the right to have an attorney present before questioning begins, and to be with you during questioning. If you cannot afford an attorney, one will be appointed for you free of charge. You also have the right to stop answering questions whenever you wish.*

*Do you understand these rights?*

*Do you want to give up your rights and answer my questions?*

If you find an officer reading "Miranda" to you, take it very seriously. It means that criminal charges are just around the corner. Indeed, you may already be in handcuffs when you hear the Miranda Warning. It's customary to "Mirandize" suspects when placing them under arrest.

In all cases, you may refuse to be interviewed, or to answer questions, under the protection of the Fifth Amendment, but only official police have to advise you of your rights. The reason is that the framers of the Constitution felt it was necessary to protect the citizen from the government, but not from other citizens.

This is why private investigators and security personnel do not give their suspects or detainees the Miranda Warning. With them, the questioning begins immediately, and often includes several intimidation tactics.

It's a common misconception that police officers always give Miranda Warnings. Not so. The Miranda Warning is required only in "custodial interrogation," which means when you're under arrest, and not free to leave. Preliminary investigations do not require the Miranda Warning. This is especially true if an investigator telephones you to obtain information. The dividing line is arrest. After arrest, you may not hear a Miranda Warning very often. For example, the officer who transports you to court, or to another jail, is not going to give you a Miranda Warning when he takes custody of you. He's also unlikely to interrogate you. However, if you voluntarily discuss your case with him, simply because you want to talk, and you make damaging admissions, don't be surprised if he reports your statements.

The basic decision regarding whether or not to talk depends mainly upon the answer to one question: "Who's got the power?" Related to this are the questions regarding what the questioner can do to you in reprisal if you keep silent, and what your goal might be.

In criminal cases, you simply can't turn around and walk out, because you're under physical or legal restraint. In other cases, such as an employment interview, you're free to refuse to answer any questions, and even leave whenever you wish, but you probably sacrifice your prospect of employment if you do.

If your employer is conducting an investigation, he may insist that you cooperate. Refusal to do this is insubordination, and you face dismissal as the penalty. In such a case, your refusal will also appear to be a sign of guilt.

If you work for a law enforcement agency, you've probably already found out that you don't have the rights ordinary citizens have. If "internal affairs" officers want to question you, or put you on the polygraph, you have no right to refuse. A Pima County, Arizona, Deputy Sheriff found this out when he became involved in a fatal shooting that was later challenged. Upon discovering that he was the subject of an investigation, he consulted an attorney, who advised him not to cooperate. He refused all interviews, and lost his job as a consequence. However, he also avoided criminal charges, and is free today. As an experienced officer, he knew that a case often hangs on the suspect's statements, and correctly calculated that it would be difficult, if not impossible, to build a criminal case without his cooperation. His choice was between being unemployed and free, or unemployed and behind bars.

In yet other cases, it's not clear. If, for example, you've been accused of a questionable self-defense shooting, you may feel that you'll make your case better if you appear open and cooperative to investigating officers. On the other hand, if you're in a jurisdiction noted for its anti-gun, anti-self-defense stance, you may be better off making no statements until your lawyer arrives.

Sometimes you have nothing to lose by stonewalling an investigation. If you're guilty, but you're the only one who knows it for sure, it's foolish to make damaging admissions.

## Keeping Your Mouth Shut Works

Competent defense attorneys know this, and advise their clients to keep their mouths shut. They know that an astute police officer can glean small details from a suspect's statement to lead him to tangible clues. Sharp attorneys also know that making statements to the media can be as damaging as speaking to the police.

Consider the case of John Carpenter, who has for many years been a prime suspect in the killing of actor Bob Crane. Crane, best known for his role as Colonel Hogan in the TV series *Hogan's Heroes,* was bludgeoned to death on June 29, 1978, in Scottsdale, Arizona. Scottsdale is normally a very quiet town, with few violent crimes. Therefore, the police department lacks experience in handling major cases. Police investigators had not done a very good job gathering and preserving physical evidence in the Crane killing, and they needed a confession to break the case. Carpenter's Beverly Hills attorney, Gary Fleischman, has advised Carpenter to refuse steadfastly to be interviewed by anyone, including the press, and to refer all questions and requests for statements to him. This policy has worked, at least keeping Carpenter out of jail during the years since the killing.[2]

Scottsdale police still suspect Carpenter, and recently failed in their efforts to obtain a DNA-typing from bloodstains found in Carpenter's rented car. Whether Carpenter actually did it doesn't matter here. The main point is that, lacking physical evidence, the only way police can obtain anything to present in court is by extracting it from the suspect directly.

## Klaus Fuchs:
## Making Something Out of Nothing

Another case was that of Klaus Fuchs, a German Communist who fled to Britain and worked on the atom bomb project during WWII. Fuchs had passed secret information on nuclear weapon design and development to Harry Gold, a member of the Rosenberg spy ring, and the FBI had discovered this only through the "Venona" code-breaking effort, which was super-top-secret. Both the FBI, and their British counterparts, did not want to reveal their cryptographic success against Soviet codes. This precluded presenting this evidence in court, or even revealing to Fuchs how they knew he was a spy.

British "MI-5" investigators decided to try to bluff a confession from Fuchs, assigning their best interrogator to the task. This was William Skardon, a former police officer who had joined up with the counterspies. On December 21, 1950, Skardon began a series of interviews with Fuchs, during which he induced him to believe that the government had a very solid case against him, and that it would be in his best interest to confess. Fuchs finally cracked, on January 24, 1951, making a full confession and cooperating in the effort to try to find his American contact. This was without any offer of immunity, which attests to the skill and persistence of William Skardon.[3]

The Fuchs case is worth studying for the lessons it teaches. The major point is that a highly skilled interrogator can bluff an intelligent suspect into a confession. Fuchs was not an illiterate street thug, but a top nuclear physicist with a life-long dedication to Communism. His interrogator, Skardon, did not work him over with a rubber hose or wet towel. He quietly and tactfully persuaded Fuchs to speak, and to make one damaging admission after another. If Fuchs had simply kept his mouth shut, the government would not have prosecuted him, because the only evidence, based on cracking Soviet codes, was too sensitive to reveal until decades after the events. The worst that could have happened to Fuchs would have been the lifting of his security clearance.

This is why, in criminal cases, the first admonition defense attorneys offer to their clients is "keep your mouth shut." They tell them outright not to speak with police officers or anyone else about the case without their being present.[4]

# Employment Interviews

Employment interviews have an important common feature with police interviews. The interviewer knows practically nothing about you, and finds out only what you list on the application form, or tell him verbally. The employment application may have a statement that you consent to a background check and understand that you may be dismissed for making false statements. However, this is usually for intimidation only, and this threat is actually illegal in some states. Employers depend very heavily on interviews and various types of tests to obtain information about their applicants. We'll explore this in depth in a later chapter.

# Resisting Interrogation:
# Basic Tactics

If ever you're interviewed or interrogated, you'll have to make a basic decision at the outset, and stick to it. You'll have to decide whether to dig in your heels and refuse to cooperate at all, or pretend to cooperate in the hope of convincing the interrogator of your viewpoint. If you cooperate, you'll need to know the tactics of interrogation so that you may devise counter-measures. The information in this book will help you decide.

# Sources

1. *Interrogation,* Burt Rapp, Port Townsend, WA, Loompanics Unlimited, 1987, p. 4.

2. *Arizona Republic,* February 11, 1990. This news article discusses only the Carpenter case, but we find corroboration in an article by Daniel D. Evans, writing in *Law and Order,* August, 1990, pp. 90-95. Evans points out that police solve most cases, by far, through interviews, and states that officers who fail to make good cases often fail because their interrogation skills are insufficient.

3. *Mask of Treachery,* John Costello, NY, Warner Books, 1989, pp. 486-490.

4. *The Mugging,* Morton Hunt, NY, Signet Books, 1972, p. 141.

# 3

# Types Of

# Interrogators

There are many types of interrogators, depending on the task and the context. Some are highly skilled professionals, while others are clowns to whom fate has given power over people's lives. The first step in calculating your chances of resisting interrogation is to understand the type of person you're facing, his level of skill, and his particular objectives.

## Police Officers

These may be uniformed officers investigating crimes and taking preliminary statements, or criminal investigators who "roll out" for special incidents. For example, robberies and homicides are always cases for plainclothes investigators, and larger police departments maintain special squads assigned to each type of crime.

Police officers handle their assignments in a routine manner, following established procedures. This doesn't mean that they're careless or stupid, but simply that they won't take any extraordinary measures to break a case. Police officers are usually as much concerned with currying favor with their superiors and avoiding lawsuits as they are with solving cases. This is not so with certain other police types.

## Special Task Force Police

Today, interagency task forces are likely to be special narcotics investigation units. These task forces contain a mixture of criminal investigators and undercover officers. Task force officers are usually volunteers bored with regular police work, and who crave the excitement of unusual assignments. A feeling of eliteness pervades special task force officers, who often have special powers and are more free-wheeling than regularly assigned officers. This promotes an arrogance that is very visible, and even a feeling that they are above the law. A task force officer is more likely to plant evidence, and to rough up a subject under interrogation, than his regular counterpart.

## Federal Agents

These run the gamut from Postal Inspectors and U.S. Marshals to the Federal Bureau of Investigation and the "hot dogs" of the Drug Enforcement Administration. Postal Inspectors and Marshals are low-key and competent, and noted for closing cases with minimal publicity. By contrast, the FBI and DEA agents tend to be more flamboyant, and some are outright publicity hounds.

Federal agencies share a characteristic with larger police departments: all have large budgets and resources. They can call upon officers who specialize in interrogation. They can also afford to conduct special interrogation courses for their officers, and even send officers to courses run outside their agencies.

## Do Police Officers Frame Suspects?

Although there are bound to be exceptions, American police officers do not knowingly frame an innocent person. Police officers, like other workers, make mistakes, but they're usually in good faith. The reason is that police officers genuinely see themselves as the "good guys," fighting a hard battle against the "bad guys," and they try to live up to their self-image.

Police officers don't, however, always play strictly by the book. They will, in certain instances, perjure themselves to help make a case against a suspect. An example is the officer who stops a known drug dealer for a traffic offense one night. He may order the suspect out of the car, and quickly search likely hiding places, such as under the seats and the glove compartment. Without probable cause, this search is illegal, and if it turns up nothing incriminating, the officer will have to let the suspect go and stonewall any complaint. However, if the officer finds a baggie of drugs, he'll have to cover himself in court by stating that he'd seen the baggie on the seat, and deny that he'd gone fishing for it.

Finally, we have the hard-core career criminal, against whom the police have not been able to make a case stick. Some police officers will, in extreme cases, frame such a suspect. Framing consists of contriving evidence pointing towards the type of crime the person normally commits. Returning to the example of the drug dealer, a simple and common way to frame this suspect is to stop him for a traffic offense, lay a baggie on the front seat of his car, and "find" it. For extra effect, the officer may also "find" a concealed weapon or other contraband when he conducts a full search after arresting the suspect.

## Private Investigators and Security Guards

Although American police officers aren't perfect, they're pretty good compared to the human material screened out during recruitment. American police officers on every level are increasingly better-paid, and receive better fringe benefits, than they did years ago. Police agencies can, therefore, be increasingly demanding in their requirements. Those whom they reject sometimes go on to become various types of private security officers.

Rejects include various types known as "wannabes," "Rambos," and other unsuitable people. A "wannabe" is a person who "wants to be" a police officer, but lacks the talent or the temperament for the job. The "Rambo" type is bloodthirsty, and entirely too uncontrolled and aggressive for police duties. The person with the "make my day" mentality is simply seeking an excuse to arrest, beat, or kill someone, and is an accident waiting to happen. Another type of person unsuitable for police work is one who actually fits into a psychiatric diagnosis, such as "sociopath," "psychotic," etc. Some of these people can marginally get along in the world, but are unsuited for any responsible employment.

Private security agencies vary from excellent to simply awful. Most pay far less than police departments pay, and cannot, therefore, maintain similar recruit standards. In other words, they hire the dregs and losers as "rent-a-cops."

Private agencies are often economically marginal operations, and cannot afford proper screening procedures. Private agency owners and managers suspect, but often don't know, that the people they hire are inept, because they don't run background checks. Instead, they rely on paper-and-pencil tests, or polygraph examinations, to screen out undesirables. This is cheap and dirty, and it shows in the results.

## Military Interrogators

Captured prisoners of war are likely to face interrogation from members of their captors' military intelligence department. These interrogators vary in quality from very good to simply awful, depending both upon their organization and whom they have captured.

Military interrogators usually work under pressure to produce quick results, information useful to the battlefield commander. They may be oriented towards humane and even gentlemanly behavior, or brutal tactics, depending again upon the standards of their organizations. Another important factor is the type of prisoner and the nature of the conflict.

Some types of prisoners, such as downed airmen who have been bombing civilians, are likely to receive harsher treatment than ground soldiers fighting against other military men. This is especially true if airmen fall into the hands of civilians and civilian organizations, such as the police. Members of some paramilitary organizations, such as the Irish Republican Army, may be surprised to find their captors treating them as criminals, instead of POWs. This is partly because the Geneva Conventions do not apply to "internal security" functions, only to conflict between nations, and partly because the occupying power does not want to legitimatize the insurgents by giving them POW status.

Certain cultures hold the belief that death in battle is honorable, while capture is shameful. Such soldiers are likely to treat POWs harshly, as the Japanese did in World War II. Likewise, members of some religions, such as the Muslims, feel that their opponents in a holy war are scum, and deserve the worst they can hand out. Torture and mutilation are routine, and anyone captured by them can expect rough treatment if they refuse to answer questions.

# Employers

Employers want to know who they're hiring, and therefore interview job applicants. Some interviews are fairly reasonable and straightforward, while others go off on tangents. Properly, the employer's business is whether you can do the job correctly. Everything else is none of his business. Regardless, there's still the "big brother" mentality among private authority figures, as among government officials. Some can't resist prying into other peoples' private business. We see this today in recent efforts to detect drug use among employment applicants. To the employer, it doesn't matter whether the job applicant uses drugs only on his own time. As long as he can get away with intrusion into the applicant's private life, he will.

There's also another side to this. An employer is concerned about the work history of anyone he's considering hiring. A problem personality or a dishonest employee is cause for concern.

There's a third side. There are people who have made mistakes during previous jobs, and who feel that they deserve another chance. There are others who have done things which, although not illegal, arouse resentment among many employers. One instance is union membership or activity. Potential employers often try to ferret out such behavior.

# Private Parties

This includes various rare types, such as criminal gangs, political extremists, etc. Right now, the chances of a citizen's being kidnaped and questioned by such a group are very small, but in countries such as Northern Ireland, this sort of thing happens almost every day. We also don't know what the future will bring. A social upheaval in ten or twenty years might see a new outbreak of vigilantism, and various other extra-legal actions. There would be informal and very violent interrogations, without any legal safeguards.

# Attorneys

Right now, conventional wisdom states that attorneys are a scruffy lot, who earn their living by misrepresenting and even cheating their clients, or by defending people who are obviously guilty. This is a simplistic viewpoint, but there are some real-life facts underlying the negative opinions many people have of attorneys. Despite the alleged shortcomings of attorneys, many people continue to employ them.

The theory of American justice is that a trial is an adversarial proceeding, with the prosecutor and defense attorney facing off and going to the mat for their sides. Although an attorney may present the appearance of doing a forceful job of representing his clients, it's mostly for show. As Alan Dershowitz has pointed out, most defendants are guilty, and everybody knows it.

If ever you face an attorney, or need to hire one, you must understand the basic fact that your attorney's first loyalty is to the system which he serves, not to you, his client. Attorneys are members of cozy little clubs, and the prosecutor is also an attorney, as is the judge. Your attorney knows that he's best off working with the judge and prosecutor, not against them. The attorney knows that he can't afford to antagonize a judge. He also knows that "he needs the prosecutor's office and that the prosecutor's office doesn't need him."[1]

Yours is only one case among many. Your attorney will have to return to face the same judge, and the same prosecutor, and he has to maintain a working relationship with them. Deep down, your attorney probably thinks you're guilty, anyway. This turns a trial into a cooperative effort, not an adversarial one.

If you hire an attorney to defend you in a criminal case, watch for one thing: Does he actually ask you if you committed the crime? If he doesn't, you can be sure that he's assumed that you did it, and that he's defending you only for the fee, or because of a belief that even guilty parties are entitled to legal defense.

In a civil case, your attorney is likely to be just as cynical, but less likely to view you as a low-life. He will take your side in court, and be with you during any deposition or hearing. Later, we'll take a brief look at what you can expect during depositions and court appearances.

## What They Have in Common

Interrogators come in different uniforms, and are from different backgrounds. Whether military or civilian, American or foreign, they tend to have certain things in common. Usually, they have similar outlooks, and similar ways of treating their subjects. We'll examine these next.

## Sources

1. *Discretionary Justice,* Howard Abadinsky, Springfield, IL, Charles C. Thomas, Publisher, 1984, p. 72.

# 4

# The Interrogator's

# Mind-Set

Anyone facing an interview or interrogation should know that interrogators, whether professional or inept, come onto the scene with certain assumptions and mind-sets. Although they make a serious effort to present themselves as "objective," they're really not objective at all. It's important to know the unspoken ground rules, and understand the hidden agenda.

## Attitude

Many interrogators adopt distinctive attitudes, which determine their tactics. Recognizing these attitudes can provide clues as to the tactics to expect.

### Everybody's Guilty

This is the extremely cynical viewpoint that affects many police officers and private investigators. They encounter so many suspects, and see so many skeletons popping out of closets, that they feel that everyone has committed some sort of crime during his life. It's easy to move from this feeling to one that suspicion equals guilt, and that suspects acquitted in court go free simply because police and prosecutors failed to find enough evidence to present, not because they were actually innocent.

### Everybody Lies

This is the corollary to "everybody's guilty." If they're not guilty of a particular offense, they're still lying about their role in the matter, because they have something else to hide.

This is also true of people who conduct employment interviews. Some feel that at least half of their interviewees exaggerate their qualifications and experience, and cover up damaging information. One serious study found that 30% of the resumes they surveyed contained "outright lies."[1] Thus the question is not whether the subject has any faults or shortcomings, but whether the interviewer can reveal them.

### Get, Don't Give

This is a standard technique used by police and other interrogators. The purpose is to reveal as little information as possible to the person being questioned, yet try to get as much as possible from him.[2] To this end, the interrogator carefully conceals what he already knows, and will even tell the subject a lie to induce him to cooperate.

One example is the questioning of a suspect's parents by a detective assigned to the Clutter murder case, popularized in the book, *In Cold Blood,* by Truman Capote. Harold Nye, the detective, interviewed the parents of one suspect, allowing them to think he was interested in their son only for fraud and parole violation. He felt that, if he'd told them he was working on a murder case, they would have been less forthcoming.[3]

Nye was cautious, but he'd already made an error that, luckily, had not compromised the investigation. He'd traveled to Las Vegas to interview the former landlady of one of the suspects, and told her that he was investigating a parole violation. She expressed disbelief that he'd come all the way from Kansas for such a petty matter, but answered his questions anyway.[4]

Having learned from this, Nye used a different tactic when he traveled to San Francisco to interview the sister of one of the suspects. Nye told her that he was "attached" to the San Francisco police, and was responding to an inquiry from officers in Kansas who were trying to locate her brother, who hadn't been reporting to his parole officer. To avoid alarming her, he didn't mention that he himself had traveled all the way from Kansas, and he never mentioned the murder investigation.[5]

Another facet of interrogation following this principle is that a successful interrogation has the interrogator contributing about 5%, and the suspect 95%. The point is to ask open-ended questions, forcing the person to provide more information.

An incompetent interrogator asks the suspect questions that he can answer with a "yes" or "no," such as: "Did you do it?," "Did you have a gun?," etc. He does most of the work, and the suspect simply denies everything.

## Criminal Types

Certain classes and certain minorities are, in the eyes of the police, more likely to be suspects than others. This is because national crime statistics show that, in proportion to their numbers in the American population, they commit more crimes.

Blacks, for example, commit a greater proportion of the violent crimes.[6] This leads police officers, who prefer to follow the main trends, to suspect members of groups often involved in crime.

Police also see certain types of people as "riff-raff," and the most likely suspects when a crime comes down.[7] A criminal record, in their view, predisposes to more crime. They also feel that many people with criminal records have committed more crimes than those with which they were officially charged.[8]

There's some justification for this belief. The clearance rate for burglaries, for example, is at an all-time low, 14%, and this includes only burglaries reported to the police.[9] According to another recent study, victims reported only 49% of burglaries to the police.[10] These figures make the bottom line very clear: Most criminals get away with many of their crimes.

This is yet more justification for the belief that suspects are lying when they're denying. A sidelight to this is the subject caught in a lie.

### One Lie Makes The Entire Statement Suspect

This is a common assumption among police and private investigators, and employment interviewers. If they catch the person in a single untruth, they assume that the person's covering up, and they discount his entire statement.

Some cynical interrogators use this to apply pressure to their subjects, by asking so many questions, about so many topics, that the subject's bound to make a mistake on one or more details. The interrogator then uses this contradiction as a lever to pry the "truth" from the subject, and to impel him to speak and reveal more information.

### Evasions Are Incriminating

A reply that doesn't answer the question directly is an evasion, in the interrogator's eyes. Saying: "I don't remember" can be construed as an evasion.

One system of linguistic analysis applicable to suspects' statements holds that, unless the subject provides a clear-cut answer, he did not answer the question. Furthermore, if he does not answer the question, he actually does, in the inference the interrogator can draw from the evasion.

### I'm Smarter Than He Is

Many types of interrogators have tremendous egos. They feel that, because of their intellect or their positions, they are superior to the people they question. At times, this superiority depends upon their using little conversational tricks, such as loaded questions, or simply on their power to approve or deny an application for employment.

All successful interrogators are fairly skilled actors. They feign surprise, suspicion, anger, and other emotions as manipulative tools to use on their subjects, while remaining in control of their emotions. At times, a raised eyebrow is more effective than an outright statement of disbelief, because it requires no explanation and no justification.

### Enough's Enough

Some interrogators will adopt a business-like, almost abrupt manner, brushing aside any denials, and insisting upon a confession. Although they won't say it in so many words, they project an attitude of: "Yeah, yeah, I know all that. Now let's get to the truth." They refuse to get involved in a discussion of alibis or denials, as if these are simply a waste of time.

One such interrogator was William W. Barnes, an investigator with the New York State Police. According to his colleagues, he had an uncanny skill of tuning in to the mind-set of his suspects, and quickly finding the key to their personalities, which he would use to make them talk.[11]

Barnes was the interrogator who cracked Marybeth Tinning, who allegedly murdered all but one of her nine children. Almost incredibly, this woman had had child after child die young, and although there were whispers and suspicions, there were no investigations, and no criminal charges, until after the death of her ninth child. Surprisingly, all deaths occurred in the same area, the city of Schenectady, New York, and its suburbs, and many people who knew Tinning knew of at least several deaths of her children. During the investigation of the ninth death, exhumations of previous dead children were unsuccessful because of extensive decomposition. This, and the lack of any direct evidence, made the case against her circumstantial. In fact, her attorney felt that, apart from her confession, "the prosecution wouldn't have a case."[12] Police strategists therefore made a supreme effort to bulldoze Tinning into a confession before she had a chance to think over her situation, and realize that she needed an attorney.

Barnes sat down with her, after she'd been questioned by other investigators, and adopted a sympathetic manner. He quietly insisted that she tell him the truth, asking her at one point, "How many more children have to die?"[13] Tinning quickly admitted her guilt, and over the next few hours, provided details to flesh out her account and make it believable to a jury.

## Body Language

Many investigators believe that body language provides clues to personality, guilt or innocence, and truthfulness. This is a trendy topic, and many police investigators attend schools that teach "kinesic" interrogation. The theory is that certain poses and gestures indicate that a subject is deceptive. Some of the poses and gestures that allegedly betray a liar are holding the chin on the chest, breaking eye contact, blinking, looking at the ceiling, and dilated pupils. Smiling is also allegedly indicative of lying, as is holding the shoulders slumped. Holding the elbows close in to the body, covering the eyes with the hands, rubbing the nose, holding arms crossed, and clasping the hands in front of the body are also alleged indicators of deception. Crossing the legs or moving the feet beneath the chair are also signs of deception, according to this theory.[14]

The importance of this body language is not that it's an accurate indicator of deception, but that an interrogator thinks it is. A nervous or timid subject who exhibits such body language will make a negative impression on an interrogator, while a practiced liar, such as one who earns his living selling used cars, can assume a confident manner, avoid making the "wrong" gestures, and appear truthful.

# Payback

This is one of the least documented aspects of police and investigatory work, but it affects investigators' attitudes almost every day. A basic rule is that of reprisal, known to police officers as "payback" or "catch-up." If, for example, a suspect resists arrest, and injures the officer, the officer will be tempted to injure him at least as much, if he can get away with it. This may happen at the site of the arrest, or in the local jail, where the suspect takes an unscheduled trip down the stairs, head-first.

Needlessly antagonizing a police officer, or even a private investigator, is a serious tactical mistake. The investigator views himself as merely doing his job, earning a living and performing a useful social function. He takes a philosophical attitude, even when he fails to make a conviction: "You win some, you lose some." To him, one suspect is much like another, unless he stands out for a special reason. Some ways in which suspects earn unwanted extra attention are:

Showing an arrogant attitude.

Making personal remarks or insulting the investigator.

Threatening him or his family.

Any physical assault.

Any of these turn the case into a personal one. The investigator will put in extra work to secure evidence and obtain a conviction. Some might even manufacture evidence. Even with a total acquittal on the charge, the suspect will face close scrutiny in the future, and be a subject of special investigation. In practical terms, this means an investigator will seek out additional violations, even petty ones, simply for harassment. It can also mean extra attention from other departments or agencies, such as the narcotics bureau, or the Internal Revenue Service.

## Ego Involvement

To an investigator, a case is a challenge to his competence, and to his ego. This is good, in the sense that it provides motivation for doing a good job. The other side is that an investigator who becomes too ego-involved loses his perspective. Some go to the extreme of seeking a confession at any price. The result is the invitation to a plea in a criminal case. The investigator bulldozes the suspect, telling him harshly that if he confesses, he'll get a reduced sentence, while if he holds out and pleads innocent, the judge will throw the book at him.

When the investigator gets to this stage, he's lost all objectivity, and doesn't care whether his suspect is actually guilty or not. The dangerous aspect of this process, as far as the suspect is concerned, is that the criminal justice system doesn't care, either. All that counts is the numbers. The prosecutor seeking a high conviction rate may offer deep "discounts" to those who make his life easier and plead guilty. The overworked judge also has an interest in seeking quick dispositions of his cases. The public defender, if you can't afford a private lawyer, is also interested in pleading his client and moving on to another case. If you're caught in such a situation, you'll be dismayed to find that nobody cares whether you're guilty or not, because you're just another obstacle they have to overcome.

## Mind-set and Its Dangers

As we've seen in this chapter, and will continue to note throughout the rest of the book, interviewers and interrogators often have an unshakable faith in their particular "system," whether it be the polygraph, linguistics, or kinesic interviewing. Whatever the system, its practitioners will tell you honestly that they've found that it works. With further probing, you may obtain an admission that the technique works most of the time, but not always. Some will even candidly cite a percentage of success, which by simple subtraction, provides a percentage of failure.

The problem comes when interrogators forget that their systems have their faults, and act as if their particular technique were infallible. Compounding this problem is the overlap between systems, so that many interviewers and interrogators are eclectic, borrowing from several different techniques. This appears pragmatic, but carries a hidden danger.

An interviewer who chooses to disbelieve his subject can find many reasons for concluding that the subject is deceptive. He may note that the subject appears nervous, and interpret that as a sign of guilt. If the subject denies guilt outright, he can dismiss this as a lie, on the basis that most are guilty, anyway. This is especially true if the subject is a minority group member. If the subject hedges his answers, the interrogator can take the linguistic approach, and conclude that, as the subject isn't answering the question directly, he's a suspect. He can also interpret a misstatement as a deliberate lie, and reject all of the subject's denials, no matter how forceful and direct they might be. One authority even states that repeated assertions of innocence are themselves incriminating.[15]

The other side of mind-set is that it blinds the interviewer or interrogator to the ones who get away with deception. The many successes are usually with people who are naive, suggestible, who lack "street smarts," and who are not career criminals. Those who succeed in deception are those who work at it, such as used car salesmen, lawyers, professional con artists, and other career criminals. These experienced deceivers are not going to fold up and tell all when faced with a polygraph test, nor will they let themselves be duped by an interrogator's bluff.

## Understanding Mind-set

When facing interrogation, most subjects arrive unprepared. A competent interviewer or interrogator makes an effort to know and understand his subject. The reverse is rarely true, which is one reason why many people fail to do well under interrogation. The pro tries very hard to "read" his subject or suspect, while the naive subject simply waits for the interviewer to make his moves. Knowing how interrogators and interviewers think, and understanding their mind-sets and motivations, is a vital basic step to resistance.

# Sources

1. *The Book of Lies,* M. Hirsch Goldberg, NY, William Morrow and Co., 1990, p. 15.

2. *Notable Crime Investigations,* William Bryan Anderson, Editor, Springfield, IL, Charles C. Thomas, Publisher, 1987, pp. 67-68.

3. *Ibid.,* p. 16.

4. *Ibid.,* p. 20.

5. *Ibid.,* p. 23.

6. *Criminal Victimization in the United States,* 1986, Washington, DC, U.S. Department of Justice, Bureau of Justice Statistics, p. 44. According to this criminal victimization survey, 24% of single-offender violent crimes were committed by black offenders, according to victims. Blacks do not comprise 24% of the U.S. population, but only about half that percentage. In multiple-offender crimes, cited on p. 49, the proportion is even higher; 32.4% all black, and 9.4% with offenders of mixed races.

7. *Notable Crime Investigations,* p. 314.

8. *Ibid.,* p. 325.

9. *Use of Forensic Evidence by the Police and Courts,* Joseph L. Peterson, Washington, DC, National Institute of Justice, U.S. Department of Justice, Research in Brief, October, 1987, p. 1.

10. *Reporting Crimes to the Police,* Catherine Wolf Harlow, Ph. D., Bureau of Justice Statistics Special Report, Washington, DC, U.S. Department of Justice, December, 1985, p. 2.

11. *From Cradle to Grave,* Joyce Egginton, NY, William Morrow and Company, 1989, p. 214.

12. *Ibid.,* p. 251.

13. *Ibid.,* p. 219.

14. *Law and Order,* August, 1990, pp. 90-95.

15. *Lie Detection Manual,* Dr. Harold Feldman, Belleville, NJ, Law Enforcement Associates, 1982, p. 181.

---

# 5

# Techniques Of

# Applying "Pressure"

---

The first task for the interrogator is persuading the subject to speak, because without active cooperation, there can be no progress for the interrogator. Police agents and other interrogators have various ways of inducing subjects to talk. Some are simple rapport and conditioning techniques, and we'll begin with these.

## Rapport

Establishing "rapport" to lull the subject is the beginning. Most people come to interviews and interrogations apprehensive, and remain on their guard throughout. One way of defusing the situation is to work hard on presenting a pleasant manner with the subject. This begins with courtesy, and continues with accepting without question everything the subject has to say.

The interviewer trying to develop "rapport" will often engage in small talk designed to show the subject that he and the interviewer have something in common. There may even be a display of feigned sympathy for the subject.

The purpose is to develop "rapport" with the subject, and it doesn't always work. Rapport is always limited because the obvious fact is that the interviewer or interrogator is not your friend! The best that the interrogator can hope for is a cautious but polite exchange, unless you fall for the phony friendliness.

## Conditioning

Conditioning the subject to answer questions is a technique that applies to all interrogations and interviews. Setting up rapport and conditioning work together to persuade the subject to "open up" and answer questions. The interrogator begins with routine, non-damaging information, such as asking the subject his name, address, telephone number, and other basic details. You can easily get taken in by this technique, because you see no harm in telling the interviewer what he already knows.

Conditioning is a powerful technique, and the interrogator will really fight to get you to accept it. If you tell him that he already has this information on file, his stock answer will be that he is simply trying to verify his information.

There's a second purpose behind asking routine questions. This is to establish a "baseline" of behavior as he notes your reactions to questions. He'll be watching your eyes, your expression, your posture, and other body language as he takes you through routine matters. Later, when the critical questions come, he'll watch for behavior changes, which according to theory denote stress. Fidgeting and changes of posture supposedly betray areas of special sensitivity.

Another aspect of conditioning is creating the expectation that the interrogator has the power to gratify or frustrate the subject. In criminal settings, an early step is to confiscate cigarettes, chewing gum, etc., and to dole them out to the subject. Satisfying hunger, thirst, and other physical needs also depends on the interrogator's consent. The purpose of these apparently petty tactics is to demonstrate that the interrogator has power over the subject.

## Intimidation

Other interrogators begin with a harder line. One technique of intimidation is for the interrogator to be seated at a desk when you enter the room. He reads a file, occasionally looking up at you with a scowl. A variation on this theme is for the person who brings you in to hand the interrogator the file, and to stand by while he reads it. This is designed to suggest that the file is about you, that it contains a lot of information, and to give you time to worry over how much the interrogator knows. It's a serious error for you to assume that the file contains anything worthwhile.

At times, the interrogator is physically much larger than the subject. This, coupled with an angry manner, can cow a subject.[1]

A very crude, but forceful, intimidation technique is to play tape recordings of people screaming outside the interrogation room. This suggests that torture will follow if no cooperation is forthcoming.

The "good guy-bad guy" technique is old, but still works. One interrogator is hard and uncompromising, while the other is gentle and sympathetic. They take turns working on you, depending on the emotional relief you experience when the bad guy leaves the room to persuade you to speak with the good guy.

## Repetition and Fatigue

Your statements provide three important possibilities to the interrogator. First is the prospect of an admission of guilt. The second prospect is providing him information he did not have before, some of which may be "leads," or avenues of further investigation. The third, and most subtle, is errors or evasions, which he can turn against you as "proof" of your guilt. Pounding away at errors and inconsistencies as signs of evasiveness can be intimidating, which is why some interrogations are lengthy.

An interrogator can wear you down by continuing the session, going over the same ground again and again. One purpose is to force you to make mistakes. Interrogators do this by insisting upon answers, even when you're not sure. You probably cannot tell the same story many times without introducing a few contradictions. Endless questioning will tire you, and phrasing the questions differently can bring forth different answers. The interrogator then uses these inconsistencies to accuse you of lying, or evasiveness.

## Verbal Tricks

There are several intellectually and emotionally dishonest ploys many interrogators use to take advantage of a subject's vulnerabilities.

### *"I just need you to answer a few routine questions."*
This approach is an effort to get you off-guard by pretending that the interrogation isn't important, but "just routine." If you

relax, and speak without thinking, you may give away something important.

You can expect the interrogator to begin with innocuous questions, such as your full name, your address, and place of employment. This is both to round out his information about you, and to condition you to answering his questions.

### *"I'm only trying to help you."*

This statement pretends sympathy for you, and for your situation. It's transparently false, as any police interrogator truly trying to help you would remove your handcuffs, open the door, and let you walk out.

### *"I want to give you a chance to tell your side of the story."*

This is a bluff often used by both police and media interviewers. It suggests that someone else has already made statements, or presented evidence, which disparages or incriminates you. The seemingly generous offer to allow you to present "your side" is only a ploy to get you to talk, in the hope that you'll provide more information which they can use to build a story or case.

If you want to expose this line of approach for its falsity, ask the interrogator outright: "Who said it about me, and what did he say?"

### *"What are you trying to hide?"*

This question contains a presumption of guilt. Anyone faced with this, or a similar question, should come right out and accuse the interrogator of asking a loaded question. Another way is to answer the question with a question: "What are you trying to make me say?"

### *"If you're innocent, you shouldn't mind answering a few questions."*

This flat statement is a contradiction of our American Constitution's Fifth Amendment regarding self-incrimination. The interrogator is telling you that your silence is proof of your guilt. You answer it by stating flatly that it's because you're innocent that you're not going to stick your head in the noose.

### *"You want to see the guilty person caught, don't you?"*

This reflexive question is another conversational trap. It is designed to put you in the awkward position of having to answer "yes" or admit that you don't want to see justice done. The way to handle this one is to reply that if the interrogator wanted to catch the guilty person, he wouldn't be interrogating an innocent person such as yourself.

### *"Please answer my questions, so we can all go home."*

Implicit in this statement is the promise to release you if you answer his questions. Don't believe it for a moment.

### *"You'll feel better if you talk to me."*

This promise of emotional relief is a gut-level effort, using suggestion. The interrogator promises an end to the unpleasant emotions you're feeling, in return for your answers, but he doesn't necessarily explain why incriminating yourself will make you feel better. Surprisingly, this suggestion works with some people. If faced with this statement, simply reply that your conscience is clear.

### *"You lied before. Why should I believe you now?"*

This is a technique of bullying used when you've made an error, or even lied, and he's caught you. It's almost inevitable, if the interrogation lasts for many hours. The best reply is a simple denial that you've lied.

## Squeezing More Information From You

Interrogators and interviewers have a repertoire of techniques and conversational tricks to get you to say more than you'd planned. Some are simple verbal ploys, based on suggestion. Others are intellectually dishonest, such as "loaded" or "leading" questions.

A basic technique is to say "and?" whenever you stop speaking. This suggests that there's more to tell. If you are suggestible, you can be spilling a lot of information under a barrage of "ands." The best response is to say simply: "That's it."

A variant on this theme is for the interviewer to say: "Now tell me the rest." You answer: "I already have."

The "predicated question" is one often used by psychologists, employment interviewers, and others who can't impose legal sanctions to pry information from you. This type of question carries an unstated assumption that you have already done something. A typical predicated question would be: "How old were you when you began to masturbate?" Another is: "Tell me about the last time you were fired."

Some are just word games, and a fairly intelligent suspect may see through them. One example is the double-bind suggestion, "Would you like to tell me about it now, or in ten minutes?" A good answer to that trick question is: "I've already told you all there is."

The single-word question is a technique used to obtain information without indicating which way the interrogator expects the answer to go. For example, he might ask you: "Where did you go yesterday?" Your answer is: "To see my friend." His one-word question would then be: "Friend?" And he'd follow this by simply staring at you, as if expecting an answer. This is an extremely economical technique of eliciting information from those who are vulnerable.

The way to reply to this is to simply repeat the word, in a positive tone: "Yes, friend." Another way is simply to nod "yes" as if to confirm that that is what you said.

## Private Investigators and Employers

As we've seen, private investigators don't have to provide a "Miranda" warning. Lacking official police powers, they also are not under the same restraints. Private investigators tend to be far more deceptive than official police. Employers are free to be more coercive. The threat of firing is a real one, and an employer can make it stick.

Of course, he cannot fire you for having committed a crime unless he has proof that you did. If he tries, you can sue him and win, but he has other grounds which make this unnecessary. He can simply order you to cooperate in the investigation, and if you refuse, fire you for insubordination.

Once you agree to cooperate, you may expect a private investigator to hammer away at you, pushing hard for information. If it becomes apparent that you're innocent, he may shift his main line of questioning to asking you who you think might be guilty. Parallel lines of questioning will cover which fellow employees use alcohol, drugs, and which gamble. Another angle is to ask you which employees you like, and which you dislike. This gives the investigator leads regarding who would be more likely to provide disparaging information about you. It also opens up opportunities to obtain disparaging information about other employees from you.

## Beyond Pressure

Interrogators and interviewers begin with mild pressure, expecting to obtain compliance and answers to their questions. Some subjects are resistant, and they have an array of deceptive tactics to employ in prying information and admissions from them. We'll study these next.

## Sources

1. *The Mugging,* Morton Hunt, NY, Signet Books, 1972, p. 97.

# 6

# Deceptive Tactics

# During Interrogation

As we've seen, many interviewers hold the attitude that their subjects are an inferior class of people, and this leads them to feel that these people therefore deserve no consideration. This is especially true of police interrogators. They have to work within the limitations of the "Miranda" decision, and a series of court decisions banning torture and the "third degree." Now that force is out, deception is in.

Other types of necessity also dictate tactics. In certain types of cases, there's no real evidence pointing to a single suspect, and solving the case depends on a skillful interrogator's narrowing the suspect list.

Let's consider industrial espionage. A bank or credit card agency may have discovered a "leak," with an employee passing authorization numbers or other confidential information to a fraud ring. The only evidence of this is a rash of unauthorized withdrawals at automatic teller machines in the area. Security officers feel that one or more employees with access to the information may have passed it to unauthorized persons. This puts everybody on the spot. In the investigators' minds, everyone's potentially guilty until proven innocent, and the only way to find out who did it is to obtain a confession. As in the Klaus Fuchs case, the only tool available is bluff.

In other cases, investigation and interrogation are merely fishing expeditions. Members of certain unpopular organizations have found themselves being investigated and interrogated by FBI agents because they did not know that they had the right to refuse to answer questions.[1]

## Bluff

Many deceptive tactics depend on bluff. The interrogator is both an actor and a salesman, and his job is to sell the subject the idea that he should confess. He can do this by selling him the idea that the interrogator already knows the truth, or that he has evidence which points to the subject's guilt. Let's look at the many forms of bluff.

### *"We already know everything, so you may as well confess."*

This is one of the oldest tricks in the book, but it can work on people who are not too bright. If you have anything better than a room-temperature I.Q., your reply should be: "If you already know everything, you don't need any more information from me."

### *"Your partner's already told us everything."*

This can be devastating if true, and a crude lie if not. The best answer is to tell your interrogator that you're not surprised, because your partner would say anything to get off the hook. You then repeat that you're innocent.

Stating that the partner has already confessed is a standard tactic, recommended by experts in criminal investigation.[2] It works because many suspects know how sleazy their companions are, and feel that their "friends" would throw them over for personal advantage.

### *"We've already got the evidence."*

Stating that they already have evidence to convict him is another deception police use to soften up a suspect. Some interrogators will even stage a fake line-up to arrange for an "identification" by someone posing as a witness. In extreme cases, they'll even accuse you of other, more serious crimes, to induce you to confess to the "real" one to get yourself off the hook.[3]

### *"Is there any reason someone would say they saw you there?"*

This is not an outright lie, but is deceptive nevertheless. It's an insinuation, a suggestion that someone saw you at a certain place, without actually saying so.[4]

The only way to handle this is to answer "no." Trying to elaborate can drag you into a swampland of discussion regarding where you actually were, and lay the way open for more deceptive tactics. A simple "no" answer tells the interrogator that he can't get a rise out of you by a shocking disclosure, true or false.

### *"They just identified you."*

Some police investigators will conduct a faked line-up, with someone playing the role of witness to point out the suspect as the perpetrator.[5] This is outright deception, but it's allowable because there are no court decisions banning police officers from lying to suspects. They may bluff as much as they wish.

The lie may take the form of a question similar to one mentioned above: "What would you say if we told you a witness said he saw you?" One answer to that is: "Tell it to me and see." Another is: "Show me the signed statement and maybe I'll be able to give you an answer." In both cases, you're politely calling the bluff.

### *"Give Them Enough Rope."*

A skilled interrogator will allow his subject to tell his entire story, without showing any disbelief, the first time around. He patiently records everything the subject says, and if he spots a discrepancy, he makes a mental note but says nothing until the end of the statement. This is the deception, intended to lull his subject, and fool him into thinking that he can slip any lie past his questioner.

### *"This is your last chance."*

Some interrogators try to gain the suspect's cooperation by stating that they have been in touch with the prosecutor, and that the suspect has an opportunity to work a "deal," *if he acts now.*[6] This is a variation of the advertising theme of "Limited time only," and is just a way to make the suspect feel a sense of urgency. In fact, such an offer holds absolutely no water unless the prosecutor signs a written agreement, preferably with your attorney present.

# The Post-test Interview

As we'll see in the chapter on the polygraph, a question-and-answer session after the test itself is often productive. Although most subjects who are going to admit deception do so before they undergo polygraph testing, some resist until afterwards. At that time, the polygraph technician tells the subject that he's having a "problem" with one or more answers, and asks whether or not the subject can tell him something more that will clear up the question.

Sometimes, this takes the form of a vague accusation that the subject hasn't told all he knows. This often happens after a written statement subjected to linguistic examination. The subject may get another questionnaire, stating that the investigator has determined that he hasn't revealed all important information, and asking him to explain this. This isn't a very strong accusation, and is designed merely to make the subject uncomfortable enough to be more forthcoming.

The same thing can happen with "honesty" questionnaires. The interviewer can state that the answers show that there is a "problem" with the subject's drinking, relations with a former employer, etc., and ask for clarification.

There are two ways to handle this sort of post-test interrogation. The first is simply to deny that there's anything more to tell. The interviewer's statement is vague enough to be meaningless, and he's not going to be able to push the issue very far.

The other way is to feign a cooperative attitude, and say something like:

"I'd like to help you. Perhaps if you could be more specific, it might jog my memory and I'd be able to help you out."

This calls his bluff immediately, and usually stifles any come-back. The word "perhaps" avoids committing you to answering.

## The Faked Ending

In non-criminal settings, deception often plays a major role. This is because coercion is not as strong, and the interviewer has to attain by guile what is denied to him by force.

A clever interviewer will often try to put the subject off guard by cueing him that the interview is "over." The purpose is to make him relax, and be less guarded in his statements. Anyone taking part in any interview, for any purpose, should be aware of these tricks, because no law can protect him against them.

One trick is to put down the pen, close the notebook, or turn off the tape recorder. The interviewer leans back, to give the impression that the session is over. This is when the interviewee should increase his alertness, because the real interview is only beginning.

There are variations on this. The interviewer may suggest taking a break. If it's lunch-time, he may suggest going out to eat, and make what passes for small talk during lunch. This is when you should be the most careful. If alcohol is available, you may have a drink, but only if the interviewer orders one for himself. If he asks you to order first, play it safe and decline the drink. Don't say that you never drink, unless you belong to a religious group that forbids drinking, or you don't drink for medical reasons. Instead, say that you have to drive, which is the currently trendy answer. This lets you off the hook even if the interviewer orders a drink himself, and forestalls the suspicion that you're an alcoholic frantically trying to deny it.

Over lunch, the interviewer may ask you some leading or loaded questions. Before answering, you have to think about his question on two different levels. First, you have to provide an answer to the question. You must also think about what he's really after with each question.

The informal questioning may start with his offering you a cigarette. You may answer that you don't smoke, which is the safe answer these days, as some companies have policies against hiring smokers. He then may mention that one of his neighbors or friends uses cocaine, and make some positive statements about this neighbor.

WATCH OUT! This is the come-on. He's implying that he approves of cocaine use, just to try to pry an admission from you. If he asks you directly if you use cocaine, just say "no." If instead he sits and stares at you, as if expecting an answer, you can say that someone you knew in college did. If he follows up with a question regarding how many of your friends use cocaine, or other illegal drugs, you can simply say "None. I don't hang around with that sort of crowd."

This is the safe answer, in Salt Lake City and most other parts of the country. In certain locales, such as Southern California and New York City, it's almost incredible that someone could reside there without having many acquaintances and neighbors who use drugs.

Another question may relate to alcohol use. If he asks you what you like to drink, you can answer that you like beer or wine with a meal. This is a safe answer, except in Salt Lake City. If your prospective employer finds any alcohol use intolerable, you have to consider whether you'd feel comfortable working for such a person.

Discussing politics is like walking blindfolded through a minefield. Be especially careful, and listen carefully to cues regarding his political beliefs. You may not be able to out-guess him unless you already know about him or his politics. Also keep in mind that he may throw out some radical ideas just to test you. The general rule is that employers aren't seeking extremists. Don't express any sympathy with the Socialist Worker's Party, the

Order, or any way-out group, unless you know for certain that your prospective employer is a member. A simple answer is to say you've never heard of the group, and that politics doesn't interest you very much.

Watch out for questions about art and literature. An interviewer may ask you if you've read any of Gore Vidal's novels, on the theory that anyone who enjoys Vidal's work must be homosexual. Likewise with authors such as Arthur Miller and Ayn Rand, who are strongly political. Miller is strongly leftist, while Rand is right-wing. Reading their works may appear to imply that you share their politics.

You might also find the interviewer bringing up other current and controversial topics, such as gun control, capital punishment, abortion, etc. These are hard to deal with directly, except for one vital point. Never, but never, get into an argument with a potential employer over politics or anything else. The purpose behind bringing up controversial subjects may well be to try to get a "rise" out of you, and to see if you're the contentious type. Businessmen seek employees who fit in, and who are team players. This means people who get along with others, not people who get into arguments easily.[7]

If an interviewer asks your viewpoint about a controversial topic, state it briefly, then shut up, especially if he contradicts you. A simple way of closing a discussion, without actually conceding, is the simple statement: "You may be right."

## Remain Alert

From this section, it's easy to see that some interrogators and interviewers can be very tricky. Some will try to make up with deception what they lack in interviewing skill. This is why it's smart to remain alert and aware, from the start of an interview until you're actually out of the interviewer's presence.

Deceptive tactics don't end with the interview or interrogation. Some interrogators are extremely sneaky, and attempt to pry information from people without telling them that they're being interrogated. We'll study covert interrogation next.

## Sources

1. *War At Home,* Brian Glick, Boston, MA, South End Press, 1989, p. 53.
2. *The Mugging,* Morton Hunt, NY, Signet Books, 1972, p. 107.
3. *Ibid.,* p. 107.
4. *Law and Order,* August, 1990, p. 92.
5. *The Mugging,* p. 105.
6. *Law and Order,* August, 1990, p. 93.
7. *Interrogation,* Burt Rapp, Port Townsend, WA, Loompanics Unlimited, 1987, p. 220.

# 7

# The Covert

# Interrogation

There are several types of covert interrogations. Some depend upon a person who does not appear to be an interrogator teasing information from the subject while he's unaware that he's being questioned.

## Pre-employment Traps

One is the fake employment candidate. During interviews, candidates wait in an anteroom to be called. One returns from his "interview," sits down next to another, and says: "Boy, that was rough! They asked me if I used drugs. I didn't admit anything. Are you going to tell them?"

# Police Informers

This is a variation of the fake prisoner trick, in which an informer is a cellmate of the suspect from whom the police need information. The informer is a criminal, promised special consideration if he obtains information useful to police.

Career criminals are a scruffy lot, and there's truly no "honor among thieves." At times, some will volunteer damaging information against another to work a "deal" for themselves. One outstanding example was Floyd Wells, a career criminal who brought information to Kansas police that was their first good lead in finding the "In Cold Blood" killers.[1] He told police about statements that his cellmates had made, as these provided leads to solving the case.

Some police agencies, such as the Federal Bureau of Investigation, make extensive use of informers. Agents assigned to criminal cases develop informers, and are constantly seeking more. FBI agents pay money for information, if it checks out, and will even have an informal word with a judge about to pass sentence. There was also a policy of unofficial tolerance for informers' criminal activities, as agents didn't investigate informers "vigorously."[2]

# False Friends

Another type of covert interrogator is the fake friend or sympathizer. This person, who may be an acquaintance, fellow employee, or neighbor, sidles up to you and tries to get you to reveal information useful to the investigation. By pretending sympathy, this type of interrogator can break down the barriers that people normally have, and obtain damaging information.

# Undercover Cellmate

This is another variant on the theme. A police officer poses as a suspect, and gets to share a cell with you. Like the genuine criminal cellmate who trades information for deals, the undercover officer will pump you for information. The chances of this happening in the future are greater, now that a court decision (Illinois vs. Perkins) has ruled that it's not necessary for an undercover police officer to give a suspect a "Miranda" warning under such circumstances. The decision went on to explain that, although "Miranda" prohibits coercion, it allows deceiving a suspect by use of a fake prisoner. The suspect is not protected against the consequences of boasting about his crimes to people he thinks are fellow felons.[3]

# Undercover Employees

An especially dangerous type is the undercover agent posing as an employee. Certain companies hire private investigators to check on employee honesty, or drug abuse in the workplace. In certain cases, undercover police officers will hire on and conduct investigations, with or without the cooperation of management.

The undercover agent poses as an ordinary employee, and tries to gain the confidence of other employees, while keeping his eyes and ears open. To succeed, he must appear competent in his work, and must have the skill to fit in and do the job. If not, he'll arouse curiosity regarding why he was hired, and why an obviously incompetent person remains in his post.

The agent will socialize with other employees as much as possible, trying to strike a mean between putting himself in a position to obtain information and not appearing "pushy." If there's a company bowling league or softball team, he'll either join or become an avid hanger-on. He'll pay special attention to cultivating talkative people, or those whose tongues loosen up with alcohol. He'll try to attend parties, to make new acquaintances, and discover weaknesses he may exploit.

You may be naive enough to think that you have nothing to fear because you're innocent. This simply isn't true, because of the secretive, conspiratorial nature of undercover work. If there's a police investigation into drug abuse, and you genuinely don't use drugs, you're not likely to be prosecuted. However, an undercover investigation takes on a life of its own, and can have other results. This is especially true if it's a private venture. A private investigator must produce results to justify his cost, and many are not beyond cutting corners to produce something to relay to their employers.

• The undercover agent may develop other derogatory information about you, which isn't criminal in itself, but which can block promotion or cause other problems for you. An example is your political philosophy. Another is membership in an organization of which management disapproves. Attending meetings of a political, social, or religious organization may get you into trouble. So can books you keep at home, and the inferences a covert investigator may draw from them. You may never know the real reason why you don't get the raise or promotion you'd been expecting, and may never even know you've been investigated.

• The agent may misinterpret something you tell him. In one case, an employee was given a bottle of brandy as a Christmas present by a vendor. Later that day, other employees saw the bottle, and asked him if he'd had a drink from it. He jokingly replied: "I always have brandy in my morning coffee." Minutes later, the company president came to confront him angrily about drinking on the job. The employee was able to show the bottle, still sealed, and explained that a certain vendor had given it to him that morning. Because there were several others present when he'd joked about the morning coffee, he was unable to pin down who had carried the word to the boss.

• The agent may try to "pump" you for derogatory information about other employees. One sidelight to this technique is to study interpersonal relationships in the workplace, and to question employees about those whom they dislike. It's easy to see that you may easily be willing to spill the "dirt" about a rival, or an abrasive personality.

Covert interrogation is very deceptive, attempting to develop information by stealth. In some situations, though, there's no attempt at subtlety, and the interrogator will proceed at once to torture.

# Sources

1. *Notable Crime Investigations,* William Bryan Anderson, Editor, Springfield, IL, Charles C. Thomas, Publisher, 1987, pp. 9-12.

2. *Ibid.,* pp. 205-206.

3. *Law and Order,* August, 1990, p. 12.

# 8

# Torture

Very few people can resist torture. Fatigue saps the will to resist, and physical torture is very fatiguing, because of the pain and the high emotional pitch of fear. Sooner or later, you'll tell the interrogator anything he wants to know. If you genuinely don't have the information he seeks, you'll make up facts to stop the pain. Even if he promises you increased pain if your statements prove to be false, at least fabrications buy you temporary relief. This is why torture is an unreliable method of obtaining confessions. Only in the most backward and despotic regimes are confessions obtained by torture admissible in court.

Another reason why physical torture is uncommon, at least in this country, is that it can produce permanent injury and even death. If you're unlucky enough to be in a situation in which you may be tortured, you risk being maimed or killed. In some countries, such as Egypt, torture is a routine part of interrogation.[1] This is why you should, if you're facing the prospect of torture, have a very clear idea regarding whether or not the pain is worth it. Are you really willing to risk being severely hurt, and even maimed, to keep the information from your questioner?

## Torture in America

However, let's emphasize that physical torture is merely uncommon, but not unknown, in this country. Various laws prohibit obtaining information by physical coercion, but a few police officers break the law. It's hard to say whether physical torture is more likely at the hands of big-city police officers, hardened by unrelenting violence, or by rural sheriffs, accustomed to imposing direct justice.[2]

Some private security agents also take short-cuts. In fact, it's more likely to happen at the hands of private security agents because these are lower-grade personnel, and usually rejects from a police employee screening program.

As a means of obtaining investigative leads, torture often works. Even if not admissible in court, information obtained under torture can help an investigation, if it checks out. This is why an interrogator will often not go too far with torture, always saving something worse for the subject who lies to him.

Some people may think that they can resist torture, because they've read of heroic secret agents resisting torture by Gestapo interrogators during World War II. According to some stories, these people went to their deaths with their lips sealed. This may have happened once or twice, but a more likely explanation is that a clumsy or cruel interrogator killed them before they could talk.[3]

Another possibility is that the subject had a severe health problem, of which his interrogators were unaware. Some types of torture are extremely stressful. The ice water bath is severe in effect, causing massive circulatory stress. A person with a heart problem may suddenly die under torture, placing his secrets forever out of reach.

# Types of Torture

There are several types of torture. The least common is physical punishment, because lesser measures will often produce information. There are also methods of physical coercion which you may not immediately recognize as torture.

### *Subtle Physical Coercion*

You can expect a short period of preparation before a severe interrogation. Your captor may allow you to drink a lot of liquids, because he knows that this will soon produce a need to urinate, which he can use to his advantage. An interrogator may not allow you to go to the toilet when you need to. If you smoke, one of the first actions of a competent interrogator is to confiscate your cigarettes and withhold them to put pressure on you. If you're a drug addict, or need regular doses of a prescription drug, such as insulin, this is another vulnerable point he'll exploit. Withholding drugs can be fatal, depending on how long the interrogator persists.

There may be a period of waiting, almost certainly in an isolation cell, while the interrogator prepares to begin on your case. The cell may be too warm, or too cold, to induce discomfort and soften you up. An hour or two of sweating or shivering will weaken almost anyone. During the interrogation, you may have to sit on a hard chair, or endure other discomforts.[4]

## Severe Physical Coercion

Many interrogators feel that results come more quickly if the subject has time to contemplate what will happen to him. This is one step beyond the initial softening-up in a hot or cold cell.

There will be a few questions to determine if you're willing to talk, and if not, there will be a few mild physical punishments. A few blows can provide a taste of things to come. More important is explaining to you what can happen, to allow your imagination to dwell on and dread the immediate future. A quick dose of psychological coercion goes hand-in-hand with physical torture.

A few simple props are often helpful. Laying some medical instruments out on a table where you can see them is a preliminary to applying torture.[5]

There are many nasty pain-producing techniques, from simple slaps and punches to exquisite technological means such as drugs and electric shocks. Every part of the body is vulnerable. Torturers pull out fingernails, twist their victim's testicles, spray them with tear gas, and pour soda pop into their nostrils.

Some techniques are based mainly on producing fear, rather than severe physical pain. Slapping or punching after an unacceptable answer is one way. Another is to tell the subject that he's about to get a lethal injection, and to actually inject morphine to produce numbness and dryness of the mouth, is another.[6] Hanging the subject upside-down and telling him that this will eventually blind him can persuade him to talk.

Some drugs cause no physical harm, but produce intense fear. Injecting a paralytic drug based on natural or synthetic curare stops breathing, without causing unconsciousness. A dose of Pavulon or Anectine, administered by a doctor or paramedic, can cause panic in a subject, who remains alert and aware, but feels himself suffocating. This has been used as a behavior modification technique in some penitentiaries.

Methods of slow torture that cause much pain before actual physical damage are desirable if it's necessary to bring the prisoner to trial, or to release him eventually. Raising the subject by tying his hands behind his back and pulling the rope over a ceiling beam causes discomfort, then pain as more weight comes off his feet.[7]

Another way is to "hog-tie" the subject, with a rope tied around his ankles and running around his neck, tightly enough so that his calves come off the floor. Relaxing his legs will apply pressure to his throat, and he'll begin to strangle.[8]

A way of producing pain without permanent physical injury is with a stun gun. This is an electronic device, costing less than $100, which produces an alternating current at 20,000 volts or more. This technique is an outgrowth of the "telephone," developed during World War II. The "telephone" was exactly that, a field telephone with a magneto-powered ringer. Spinning the crank would generate a high-voltage current, which the interrogator would apply to the subject's body. Modern electronics provides high-voltage current from a 9-volt transistor battery and a small circuit board.

The stun gun has two contacts, or probes, to carry the current to the skin. A jolt from a stun gun causes intense pain, but leaves no marks, unless the user is careless and allows a gap between the electrodes and the skin. Sparks can burn the skin.

Stun guns have been used to persuade suspects to talk. In one case, in early 1985, a sergeant and a patrolman of the New York City Police Department's 106th Precinct used a stun gun on two drug dealers to elicit information. This was the noted "Torture Precinct" incident, and both officers earned prison sentences for their acts.

These electric torture devices are very different in use from electric-shock machines used in psychiatry. Psychiatric electro-shock involves passing a current through the frontal lobes of the brain, to produce unconsciousness and convulsions. The effects can be moderate to severe, with confusion and loss of memory almost always resulting from each treatment. This is why psychiatric electro-shock is useless for interrogations. Today, its use is limited to treating some cases of depression, and for discipline and control of unwilling subjects. Some backward mental hospitals, as well as some prisons, use intensive shock treatments to make difficult and combative inmates docile and manageable.

Another way of producing intense discomfort is by placing a rag soaked in household ammonia over the face. New York City police sometimes use this technique.[9]

You may be subjected to one or more of these physical techniques, and unless your interrogator is totally inept, they'll be in a definite order. Least harmful techniques come first, with more severe and damaging methods later. The point is to produce information with the least physical damage, and no maiming, if the plan is to release you. If you find your arms and legs being broken, or your eyes gouged out, you can be sure that you're not coming out of the ordeal alive.

Torture is not the best way to obtain information from a suspect, partly because it's legally doubtful, but also because it's unreliable. There are, however, technological means of interrogation, such as the "lie detector." We'll see how this works next.

# Sources

1. *A Handbook For Spies,* Wolfgang Lotz, NY, Harper & Row, 1980, p. 118.

2. *The Mugging,* Morton Hunt, NY, Signet Books, 1972, p. 106. The case described is that of three Southern Blacks, illiterate and suspected of murder, whom local sheriff's officers had whipped repeatedly until they confessed. This 1936 case, Brown vs. Mississippi, resulted in the U.S. Supreme Court reversing the conviction on the grounds that the suspects had been deprived of their rights without due process by the torture.

   In another case in the same book, described on p. 113, a New York police investigator clamped a rag soaked in ammonia over the suspect's face, forcing him to inhale the fumes until he lost consciousness. The "third degree" is not totally gone from American policing.

3. *Handbook For Spies,* p. 117.

4. *The Mugging,* p. 107.

5. *Elementary Field Interrogation,* Dirk von Schrader, El Dorado, AR, Delta Press, 1978, p. 24.

6. *Ibid.,* pp. 25-26.

7. *Ibid.,* p. 31.

8. *Ibid.,* pp. 34-35.

9. *The Mugging,* p. 102.

# 9

# The Polygraph

The polygraph evolved during the early years of this century, following the pioneering work of an Italian anthropologist and criminologist, Cesare Lombroso, who had measured blood pressure and pulse rate during interrogation. Several other individuals devised instruments to record heartbeat, blood pressure, breathing and even electrical resistance of the skin, as a guide to determining truthfulness. At the time, the assumption was that disturbances in these would occur if the subject told a lie.

## Early History

In 1921, John A. Larson brought out the definitive version of the "polygraph," and his supporters promoted it as a "lie detector." Another notable person in this field was Leonarde Keeler, who improved the device and popularized it through the media. He had a weekly radio show during the 1940s, and made a personal appearance in the film, *Call Northside 777,* to bring his machine before the public. The audience had an opportunity to see a subject with ribbed tubing and wires attached to his chest and arms, all connected to a machine that unrolled a long strip chart that recorded the readings in a series of wavy lines.

The net result is that the polygraph attained wide acceptance in the gadget-happy United States, not because of its merit, but because of public-relations hype. The picture presented to the public was of a scientific and objective instrument that would reliably disclose whether a person was being truthful or not. Several schools sprang up to train polygraph operators, teaching them not only how to operate the device, but also a battery of tricks to use in intimidating subjects. One trick, for example, is to hook up the subject to the machine, and tell him that the charts will disclose if he lies. The operator then lets the subject pick a card from a deck, and the operator asks him if it's the ace of hearts, two of hearts, etc., with the subject answering "no" to each question. After several questions, the operator informs the subject what his card is, implying that the machine spotted the deception. The trick is that the deck used in this stunt is a "force deck," made up of fifty-two identical cards.

## How It Works

The polygraph's strip chart records pulse, respiration, blood pressure, and galvanometric skin resistance. If the pulse and blood pressure increase, respiration loses its regularity, and skin resistance drops. These symptoms indicate stress, and the operator interprets this as deception.

All questions in the series require only a "yes" or "no" answer. The operator will usually read the questions to the subject before the actual test, to start him anticipating and worrying.

The operator asks the subject a series of questions designed to both establish a baseline for the charts, and to measure the subject's reaction to critical questions. "Neutral" questions are routine questions designed to be emotionally neutral, such as "Is your name John Doe?" or "Do you live in New York?" The recordings for such questions establish a level of response for normal questions that don't place the subject under emotional stress.

"Control" questions are designed to evoke deceptive answers. The purpose is to obtain a high-stress baseline, for comparison to questions relevant to the investigation. Examples are:

"Did you ever masturbate?"

"Did you ever steal anything?"

The operator may not, at the outset, know whether the subject masturbated, stole anything, or committed any other specific acts. He can, however, develop a set of control questions by simply asking the subject if he ever committed any of these acts, and then instructing him to answer "no" to the questions during the actual test.

Relevant questions relate directly to the investigation. They may simply take the form of "Did you do it?" but many operators prefer to use a more complicated format. One is called the "SKY" sequence. This acronym stands for "Suspect," "Know," and "You."[1]

A typical sequence of questions reads:

"Do you suspect anyone of the crime?"

"Do you know for certain who committed the crime?"

"Did you commit the crime?"

Exact phrasing will vary with the investigation. The questions, in an arson investigation, might all end with "... set the fire?"

Another type of sequence design is the "peak of tension" test. The operator asks the subject questions rotating around the topic, and notes the highest responses. In a theft case, for example, he may ask:

"Is the missing amount between $1,000 and $2,000?"

"Is the missing amount between $2,000 and $3,000?" etc.

The guilty party will presumably have the strongest reaction after the operator mentions the correct amount.[2]

Questions are spaced out, with several seconds between them, to allow clear readings of the subject's reactions to each. There will often be neutral questions between relevant and control questions, to get a reading on the subject's overall level of tension.

There may be other questions, to probe the periphery of the investigation. One way to explore other areas is to ask:

"Have you been concealing any information from me?"

Other questions used to probe are:

"Is there anything you stole that I haven't asked you about?"

"Have you been truthful in all your answers?"

"Do you have any knowledge of other acts that we didn't cover here?"

"Have you lied in any of your answers in this test?"

"Have you withheld something important?"

Polygraph operators usually follow up the test with a post-test interrogation.[3] In theory, this is to point out areas of strong responses on the charts, and to offer the subject an opportunity to explain them. In reality, this is another way of badgering the subject into a damaging admission. Some polygraph operators routinely bluff every subject this way, whether or not the charts indicate deception at all.

In some cases, the operator will tell the subject that, while he appeared to have answered the relevant questions truthfully, he showed reactions to some control questions. The pitch then goes like this:

"Just for my own curiosity, can you tell me what you did steal?"

Questions such as these open the door to further interrogation. This is why it's important to be on your guard until you've left the building. The interrogation isn't over until it's over.

## How Reliable is the Polygraph?

Most courts don't admit polygraph charts as evidence, because despite various stunts displayed by some polygraph operators, the device's reliability remains unproven. In 1988, Congress passed the Employee Polygraph Protection Act, sharply limiting the use of the polygraph in private employment practice. Up to this point, some companies had subjected all employment applicants to polygraph examinations, as part of the screening process. Using the polygraph had been a cheap substitute for background checks, which can be very costly. Employment managers felt that it was enough to carry out a superficial check of easily verifiable details on the employment questionnaire, and ask the applicant to state under polygraph examination that he had answered all questions truthfully. Some companies also required applicants to sign consent forms, to allow polygraph examination whenever management thought it appropriate. One chain of convenience stores, for example, had a policy requiring polygraph examinations of employees immediately after any robbery. Clerks on duty during the robbery would find that they were automatically the top suspects, and be obliged to report for polygraph examinations.

Police and other investigators continue to use it, because they know it has some value in intimidating naive and credulous subjects who can be fooled by card tricks. In fact, most of the polygraph's successes come before the actual test, when the subject confesses, rather than allowing himself to be hooked up to the machine.

Police agencies use the polygraph to screen applicants, as a supplement to the background check. This is supposedly an additional safeguard against unsuitable people becoming police officers. However, even the multi-layered applicant screening process doesn't always work.

One police chief of a small Arizona town, exposed as an impostor, had passed a polygraph examination to get his job. He had claimed both military and police experience he did not have, and exaggerated his educational accomplishments. The polygraph operator passed him anyway. The recent case of an Arizona Highway Patrolman, who persuaded a motorist to have sex with him to avoid a traffic ticket, involved an officer who had passed both a polygraph examination and psychological screening before hiring. The Arizona Department of Public Safety placed great faith in these tests, but found that they have their limitations. These cases are only the tip of the iceberg, and there are many other examples waiting to surface. Today, practically all persons applying for police employment must take screening tests or polygraph examinations, and sometimes both. It's worth remembering, whenever a case of a "bad cop" surfaces, that the officer involved is probably another polygraph failure.

One outstanding case of failure was the polygraph testing done on Robert "Bud" Mcfarlane, President Reagan's National Security Advisor when an article suggesting a leak appeared in the *New York Times*. It seemed that someone in the White House had passed restricted information to the newspaper, and several staffers with access to this information had to take polygraph examinations. Mcfarlane took the test twice, failing each time, and it appeared that he was the guilty party. He begged the *New York Times* management to tell his boss, the President, that he had not been the one who had leaked the information. The *Times'* publisher told President Reagan that their information had not come from Mcfarlane, and this cleared his name.[4]

This case is worth studying further, because it holds several lessons regarding how and why the polygraph "works," and shows plainly the problems with the system. First, we can see that anyone who cares about his job and his career will find an accusation of criminal malfeasance very stressful. His pulse and blood pressure will go up when discussing the accusations, whether he's in fact guilty or not. This is also true of people accused of crimes with strong emotional content. Anyone accused of child molesting, for example, is likely to find it very disturbing. A polygraph operator looking for disturbance in the lines on his graph won't have much difficulty in such cases.

The blunt fact is that the polygraph measures the physical results of emotional stress, not truthfulness or deception. The results of polygraph tests are also often not as clear as its proponents claim. If there are many suspects, for example, the polygraph will not zero in on a single person, but the tests will usually result in a short list of "probables." These are people who showed some stress on the charts during the questioning. It also doesn't necessarily follow that the person who showed the most deviant readings is the one most likely to be guilty.

Why, then, do police agencies and various private investigators continue to use the polygraph, and insist that it works? In one sense, the machine does work. Many subjects, when faced with a polygraph examination, will make damaging admissions before the start of the test, because they think that they'll be found out, anyway. They don't know or understand the severe limitations of the polygraph, which is why they get bluffed out. About 75% of employment applicants required to take polygraph examinations made damaging admissions before the start of the test.[5]

In one case, an estranged wife accused her husband of sexually molesting their son. The husband asked for polygraph examinations of both of them, and the day before the scheduled tests, the wife confessed that she had fabricated the accusation.[6]

## Fooling The Polygraph

This task has two aspects: fooling the machine itself, and fooling the operator. We'll look at fooling the machine first.

A person intent on deception has several ways to pass a polygraph examination. A person who is particularly nervous or apprehensive can also benefit by studying these methods, because the polygraph, as we've seen, does not discriminate between anxiety and deception.

One quick way to appear less apprehensive, and to blunt the emotional responses, is to take a tranquilizer an hour before appearing for the test. All competent polygraph operators ask their subjects whether they're taking any drugs, prescription or otherwise, because they know that someone under "chemical control" won't respond as intensely to stimuli. This is why, if you're apprehensive about taking a "lie detector" exam, you pop a pill and begin with a lie, denying that you're taking any drugs at all.

One popular tranquilizer that works well for this purpose is Valium. Doses range from two to ten milligrams, but the most effective dose appears to be ten mg. on an empty stomach.[7] You can ask your doctor for a prescription, stating that you feel nervous, and there's a better than even chance that he'll write you a prescription for what you ask. This is especially true if you ask him for only half a dozen, stating that you feel nervous only occasionally, and that you'd previously found that Valium works well for you. He's less likely to insist on another drug, because of the small amount and your purported beneficial experience with Valium.

Another drug recommend by an authority on beating the box is Elavil, in doses of 5-75 mg. There were, however, some side effects, including some loss of coordination and concentration.[8] An alert polygraph operator might notice these.

If you're lucky, you can scrounge a couple of pills from a friend or relative. Either way, you have to find the correct dose for you. This means testing the drug on yourself a couple of days before you take the test, to make sure that it calms you enough, without inducing dizziness or any signs that a polygraph operator might detect. If your only transportation is a car, it's also important that the dose you take isn't heavy enough to impair your ability to drive.

Alcohol will do, if you're in a hurry and have nothing else. If you use alcohol, drink the least aromatic form you can find, which is vodka. If you find the taste of pure vodka too sharp, dilute it with water, orange or tomato juice, or even milk. Chewing gum will mask the slight odor of alcohol on your breath.

Relaxation exercises can also work to reduce stress responses. However, they take time to learn, and practice is essential.[9]

There have been various "biofeedback" devices appearing on the market in recent years. These are solid-state devices to measure pulse, skin resistance, etc., and they can help you monitor your physiological responses to questioning. The main difference between these and polygraphs is that they make no permanent record.

Flattening stress responses is one approach. Heightening responses to neutral and control questions is the other. You can practice several techniques to boost your blood pressure and heart rate upon demand. The thumbtack in the shoe is very well-known, which makes it obsolete.[10] Experienced polygraph operators will be watching for this, and scrutinizing you carefully to see if you walk with a limp, or favoring one foot, a tip-off that you have to be careful how hard you step.

The best ways are those requiring no gimmick at all. Biting your tongue, tightening your crotch or sphincter muscles, and voluntarily holding your breath are all ways of heightening your responses to neutral and control questions. Do not use muscular tension that the polygraph operator can see, such as gripping the arms of the chair, because he'll be watching for these tricks.

## Fooling the Technician

Fooling the machine is only one step. You also have to put yourself across properly to the person who gives you the test. To do this, you have to present the appearance of being both truthful and cooperative.

There are two theories of scoring the polygraph test. One school of thought goes only by the chart, on the assumption that the needle tracings tell all. This allows an expert to interpret the charts of a subject he's never seen, and arrive at an opinion regarding the person's truthfulness.

The other theory is what practitioners call "global scoring." The technician looks not only at the charts, but at the subject's general behavior. Subjects who arrive late, for example, indicate to the operator that they're being uncooperative, and therefore suspect. So do subjects who express skepticism, such as doubting that the machine works. Those who break eye contact, stare at the ceiling, appear nervous, and exhibit other signs of lack of confidence also appear suspicious. Expressing resentment at being required to take the test is also an indicator of deception, the way these people think.

Other techniques which supposedly indicate deception are the "red herring," in which the subject begins arguing the unfairness of the suspicion, accusation, or the test itself. Another type of incriminating statement is arguing over petty details, and claiming that, because there's no proof of every detail, then the subject must be totally innocent. Attacking a witness's motivation or integrity is another tactic, according to this school of thought. Starting extraneous conversations is also another deceptive or obstructive tactic.[11]

Weaseling statements are also cause for suspicion. These usually take the form of not quite answering a question:

Q: "Did you do it?

A: "People will tell you that I'm innocent."

This is not a denial of guilt, but an indirect statement that other people will confirm innocence. Deceivers also pepper their answers with other weaseling qualifiers, such as: "...to the best of my knowledge..." or "...as far as I remember..." Others will answer a question with a question, such as: "Who, me?" or "Are you calling me a liar?"[12]

This is why you should be punctual and show the technician a cooperative attitude. Don't express any doubt or resentment regarding the test, his qualifications, or the fairness of the procedure. Act as if you're a totally innocent person, with nothing to hide. However, the best you can do may not be enough. Global scoring is so intuitive, and so imprecise, that an operator who has already made up his mind about you can find a lot of material to justify his beliefs.

One countermove is a clever play for sympathy. A man applying for a security job had apparently made the needles jump when asked if he had a problem with alcohol. In the post-test interview, the technician confronted him with this, and asked him if he had any explanation for it. The reply was that he'd only the day before heard that his uncle, who had been an alcoholic, had died from cirrhosis of the liver. He passed.

The polygraph is cranky and unreliable. So is the "voice stress analyzer," fashionable a few years ago but now passing out of use. This machine allegedly detected lies by changes in the lower frequencies of the voice, but turned out to be so unreliable that it never attained even the limited acceptance of the polygraph.

# Sources

1. *Lie Detection Manual,* Dr. Harold Feldman, Belleville, NJ, Law Enforcement Associates, 1982, pp. 111-114.

2. *Ibid.,* pp. 116-119.

3. *Ibid.,* pp. 174-175.

4. *The Book of Lies,* M. Hirsch Goldberg, NY, William Morrow and Co., 1990, pp. 232-233.

5. *A Tremor in the Blood,* David Thoreson Lykken, NY, McGraw-Hill, 1981, p. 238.

6. Related personally to the author by the intended victim.

7. *How To Get Anything On Anybody,* Lee Lapin, San Francisco, CA, Auburn Wolfe Publishing, 1983, p. 213.

8. *Ibid.,* p. 213.

9. *Interrogation,* Burt Rapp, Port Townsend, WA, Loompanics Unlimited, 1987, p. 107.

10. *Ibid.,* p. 107.

11. *Lie Detection Manual,* pp. 174-182.

12. *Ibid.,* pp. 183-185.

# Part II:

Special

Applications

# 10

# Prisoners

# Of War

Prisoners are valuable to their captors because of information they may provide about the enemy's strength, weapons, casualties, morale, and even plans. This is why standard practice is to set up a system of interrogating captives.

## Rights of Prisoners of War

According to international law, POWs have certain "rights," but only under certain circumstances. There have been several Geneva Conventions, all directed towards defining the status of POWs, and the treatment they receive by participating nations.

If you're a military person captured by enemy forces, the treatment you may expect will vary depending on several conditions. The Geneva Convention is not universal, and not all nations in the world have signed it. Historically, nations which have provided the most humane treatment to POWs, partly because they are signatories and partly because of tradition, have been the Western nations. We're not likely to be at war with Britain or France in the foreseeable future, and may instead be fighting in the Middle East or Asia. Nations which have not signed the Geneva Convention have their own rules, and generally they treat POWs harshly.

Another condition is whether or not there's a declared war. American fliers shot down over North Vietnam were surprised and dismayed to find their captors telling them that, as the United States was not at war with North Vietnam, they did not qualify for POW status. Instead, they carried the label of "criminal." If you're captured during an undeclared "police action" or other type of intervention which is not a fully declared war, your uniform may not protect you.

The Geneva Convention applies only to war between nations, not to internal security functions, police actions, or civil wars. If you're involved in one of these, don't be optimistic about your prospects if captured.

It also applies only to members of the armed forces in the sense that they are the only ones allowed to fight under its terms. Civilians are non-combatants, and as such, they're not allowed to take up arms against the enemy's armed forces. A set of rules governs treatment of civilians, who are not allowed to be used for military labor, as hostages, etc. Any civilians who fight, in a guerrilla or underground movement, forfeit their rights under the Geneva Convention. If you're a civilian fighting against an occupation army, expect them to treat you as a criminal if they capture you.

This is true of any nation, even the ones we consider very civilized. In Northern Ireland, members of the Irish Republican Army do not get POW status when captured. On the contrary, they get put on trial for their "crimes," as if they were street criminals. In the United States, members of various "liberation armies" have faced trial and imprisonment upon capture.

Certain practical conditions also affect what you may expect if captured. If you're a flier who has just been bombing the enemy's homeland when shot down, you may face some very angry people who may not be at all interested in your information, only your blood.

## Military Interrogation Goals

There are many purposes to military interrogation. The most important and universal one is to squeeze you for information. You may face questions about your unit, officers, weapons, tactics, and other details of your organization. This is "front-line" or "tactical" intelligence, which is information immediately useful to the battlefield commander.

There are also longer-range objectives, such as forming strategic estimates of morale of your armed forces, or morale and will to fight in your country. This is information that isn't as urgent, and is the concern of interrogators at POW camps.

Another purpose is to use POWs for propaganda. A few POWs who sign a declaration that the war is unjust can generate favorable propaganda for their captors. POWs who sign confessions of atrocities can also help their captors.

## Military Interrogation Tactics

There are several types of military interrogations, for different purposes and locales.

"Field Interrogation" is to obtain immediately useful information. You may, if captured, expect this within a few minutes or hours of being taken prisoner. An intelligence officer will question you in a dugout or tent, not far behind the lines, to get what he can as quickly as possible. He may simply question you, or may threaten force if you remain unresponsive. You may face a severe beating, with broken teeth and bones, or a quick execution, if you don't cooperate.

"Shock Interrogation" overlaps with Field Interrogation. Here, the theme is speed, to put questions to you while you're still shocked by your capture, and before you can regain your mental balance and begin adjusting to captivity. An important part of shock interrogation is to keep you isolated, especially from countrymen who have also been captured, to deny you mutual support. Once you're in a camp with other captives, the value of shock interrogation is far less.

"Interrogation by Deception" takes many forms. An enemy may pose as an officer in your armed forces, to question you regarding your activities before capture. You may find enemy officers handing you a "Red Cross Form," to allow them to notify your family that you're alive and well, although a prisoner. The form contains many questions not relating to your family, but instead covering military information.

Some interrogators use "killing with kindness." This involves simply being nice, thoroughly solicitous of the POW's needs, and being consistently polite. The interrogator may wear a uniform of the corresponding service, but a grade higher than the POW. The session does not begin with an interrogation, but as an invitation to tea or dinner. Small talk over the meal produces relaxation, and may lower the POW's guard. As a fellow sailor, or airman, the interrogator can discuss service matters professionally with the POW, and by gradually leading the conversation around to military topics, may be able to obtain the information he seeks. This technique served both British and German interrogators well during the last global war.

Once you're in a formal prison camp, you'll be under several different types of pressure from your captors, aimed at getting your cooperation in several different ways. Some tactics will also deal with alienating you from your buddies, to keep you emotionally isolated.

Another set of tactics involves necessities and amenities of life. If you're wounded, your captors may tell you that medical care is rationed, and available only to those friendly to the regime. They may offer you medical care in return for your expression of friendliness, in the form of information or a confession.

Physical discomfort can break down both morale and health quickly. One harsh tactic is to keep the POWs in small cells or boxes, without food or water, for several days at a time. Forced to sit in their own excrement, they soon weaken and become ripe for interrogation based on a system of rewards.[1]

Food, clothing, and heating fuel are also media of exchange. You may find the prison camp diet inadequate, and learn that you can earn an adequate ration by cooperating with your captors. In cold climates, you'll find your barrack room cold, and you won't have enough blankets, unless you give your captors what they want. Mail to and from home is also a medium of exchange, and you might find that only letters which contain statements favorable to the regime ever reach your family. Your captors might also withhold mail from home, until you agree to cooperate.

"Salami Slicing" is a variation on the theme. Your captor doesn't try to get you to provide information or to sign a confession immediately, instead offering rewards to those who attend an "orientation" lecture. This is in a comfortable room, and he serves refreshments after the lecture. He may follow this with a "study" period next day, with rewards to those who can pass a test on the topic studied. The rewards continue, and each step in cooperation is so small that it's hard to draw the line and begin refusing.

All of these are proven techniques based on principles of behavior modification. They don't work equally well with everybody, but they work.

## Tactics For Prisoner Management

Prison camp administrators need to keep their captives docile and compliant, to help the interrogators with their job. They do this by using several means to lower their captives' morale.

"Managing the News" is common. The camp administration controls all news arriving in camp, especially news from home, to keep the prisoners feeling isolated and forgotten. If an armistice is imminent, the prisoners don't hear about it, unless it serves a purpose for the interrogators.

Suborning prisoners is also common. In any group, some are stronger than others. Camp administrators seek out the weakest ones, and apply intense pressure to obtain their cooperation. This gets a foot in the door, and other POWs who see a few benefiting from cooperation may also be tempted.

Breaking the chain of command is another tactic to reduce prisoner morale and cohesiveness. When camp administrators see group leaders emerging among the prisoners, they transfer or kill them. Officers are not allowed contact with the men, and regular executions prevent the development of any sort of prisoner organization.

Cultivating informers is especially valuable, because few things break down morale as quickly and thoroughly as knowing that someone wearing the same uniform is betraying you. The most important part of such a program is letting the prisoners know that their words and actions are the subjects of reports to the administration from within their own ranks. Letting a few tid-bits of information slip is one way to increase anxiety.

Another is developing a fake informer. This works if prisoners regularly face interrogation and beating. The administration selects several who are particularly hostile and uncooperative, and calls them in for "interrogation," one at a time. Instead of suffering questioning and beating, they simply sit in a room alone for a couple of hours. At the end, each gets a chocolate bar or pack of cigarettes, and is allowed to leave. Other prisoners will quickly notice that some come out of interrogation sessions without any marks or bruises, and with small gifts. This creates suspicion quickly.

## Surviving POW Interrogation

American servicemen have to obey a code of conduct, which prohibits giving an enemy useful information, or cooperating in any action harmful to the United States. This originated after the Korean War, during which American servicemen in Communist hands embarrassed their government by signing confessions and denouncing American war aims. 7,190 Americans spent time as POWs during the Korean War. 2,730 died in captivity, and of the survivors, 13% collaborated with their captors, some giving in after only a few minutes.[2]

The code of conduct requires American servicemen to continue fighting while they still have the means to resist, try to escape if captured, and to avoid saying or doing anything that would benefit the enemy. They must not provide any information beyond their name, rank, and serial number, and must not give their "parole" that they won't try to escape. POWs also must maintain a chain of command, and obey their superior's lawful orders.

The problem with this code of conduct is that the people who wrote it, and who require American servicemen to follow it, are not the ones behind the barbed wire. It's easy to sit behind a desk and write regulations that cold and starving men thousands of miles away are supposed to obey. In practice, human resistance can go only so far. The experiences of POWs in Vietnam showed the limits.

In a short war, with POWs in captivity for only a few weeks or months, morale doesn't suffer as much, and it's easier to resist when your health is still good and you expect release soon. Your captors, as well, probably will be mindful of the prospects of retaliation if they mistreat you. If the war lasts for years, with poor food, no news from home, and no prospects for release, your morale will suffer greatly.

It's even more difficult if you're injured. Physical injury is weakening, and recovery is longer and more difficult on a marginal diet.

There are still some survival measures you can take. One is to discard rank badges, and try to pass for an enlisted man if you're an officer. Enlisted men, in principle, have less information than officers, and this may spare you some intensive interrogation.

Important to survival is your awareness of the tricks enemy captors may use against you. Trust in your fellow prisoners is very important, and you must be aware of the ways the enemy will try to divide you by creating distrust. At the same time, it's important not to discuss classified military matters with fellow prisoners. They don't need to know the details of any secret equipment you operated before capture, and anyone who tries to get this information from you may be a plant or an informer.

It's also wise not to draw any conclusion about informers without proof. Some may appear to be collaborating, or passing information, but an accusation of treason can be devastating to camp morale.

Don't try to hold your own courts-martial and executions of those whom you suspect of treason. It's illegal under the Geneva

Convention, and the enemy can put you on trial as a common criminal. Save your testimony for later, after you're back home, and tell what you know to your superior officers. It then becomes their problem, and they'll have the resources to handle it.

Finally, you must understand that there are some situations which you won't be able to handle. An example is being taken as a civilian engaged in sabotage or resistance. Military Intelligence, or the civilian secret police, will be able to do what they want with you, including execution without trial.

## Sources

1. *Interrogation,* Burt Rapp, Port Townsend, WA, Loompanics Unlimited, 1987, p. 190.
2. *Techniques of Persuasion,* J.A.C. Brown, Baltimore, MD, Penguin Books, 1963, pp. 283-284.

# 11

# Pre-Employment

# Interviews

These interviews are among the more stressful experiences Americans undergo, except for the hereditary rich, who don't need to work. Despite the vast number of pre-employment interviews personnel managers conduct each year, some remarkable fakers slip through the process.

One of the most notable fakers was Ferdinand Demara, Jr., who faked his way into several high-level jobs in the United States and Canada. He became a Canadian Navy doctor, professor at Pennsylvania's Gannon College, law student, zoology graduate, teacher, and a monk. His career was so outlandish and remarkable that Hollywood made a movie about him, starring Tony Curtis.[1]

Let's look at the pre-employment screening process, which involves several stages. Getting a job is truly running the gauntlet, with a series of obstacles to overcome.

## Posture

Remember a few basics about job-seeking. These will direct your answers to certain questions, and help you to be consistent. We'll call this your "posture." Use it as a guide when tailoring your answers for specific employers:

You are competent. You can do the job. Other employers have paid you because you did the job well for them.

You have suitable qualifications for the job you're seeking, which means not too many and not too few. If the job requires a college degree, you must state that you have one. By contrast, don't appear "over-qualified," as this will block employment. In fact, an employer might wonder why someone with a master's degree is seeking a job frying hamburgers. The practical point is that the employer will feel that you'll work for him only until you can find something better.

You generally get along well with other people. You do not have personality clashes or conflicts with fellow employees or with supervisors.

You express a positive attitude towards former employers and supervisors, demonstrating this by praising them. This shows that you got along well with them.

Your career has been upward and onward. Each job you left was for more money and benefits. Each job should reflect more income. The exception is if you were laid off, or your employer went bankrupt. In such cases, it's reasonable to accept the same or less pay, just to get a job.

You are normally cheerful, and don't have any serious problems, mental or physical. You also do not worry much.

You are outgoing, and prefer activities that bring you into contact with other people. You prefer bowling, for example, over stamp collecting.

Whatever you do, don't allow yourself to feel intimidated or discouraged. Remember that you're competing for the job, but not usually against the cream of the crop. No matter how much puff a prospective employer puts out about his company's high standards, and how he hires only the best, the fact remains that if he paid enough, he'd already have the best working for him. You're only competing against a limited field.

# Resumes

This isn't a chapter on how to write resumes, because you can obtain that information from other books. Instead, it's going to deal with the uses of a resume, and make you aware of certain pitfalls.

You can use a resume for two purposes:

1. As a door-opener to mail to prospective employers. This is routine, and often a waste of time unless you're responding to a specific classified ad or other indication that there's an opening.

2. As a crib sheet when filling out employment applications. Wait a minute! If you present a resume, why would an employer want you to fill out an additional form?

The reason is that most resumes don't tell an employer what he wants to know about you. A "functional resume" lists your skills, but doesn't go into detail about your employment history. In the same manner, a "chronological resume" lists your employers, but is unlikely to list how much you earned at each job, or your reasons for leaving each. Employers want this information, and you can be sure that they'll ask you.

Another reason is that many resumes are carefully edited versions of the truth, designed to make you look as good as possible, while concealing weaknesses and vulnerabilities. Many people puff up their careers in their resumes, which is why many employers and their personnel managers feel that 50% of a resume is bullshit.

One form of "faking good" is the "Apollo Syndrome." The name comes from the person who served the coffee to scientists and engineers at Cape Kennedy during the Apollo launch, and who claims credit for its success because his coffee kept them awake to do their jobs.[2]

Employment interviewers also look for puffed up language, such as "implemented" and "directed." These may mean that the applicant was in charge of an important program, or that he simply shuffled papers. To avoid suspicion, use simple language that directly describes your responsibilities in each job.

Also avoid listing diplomas from obscure colleges, unless they're real and you have a copy with you. There are many diploma mills in this country, and employers are wise to this trick.

One way of scoring points is to state that former employers sent you to training courses and seminars. This shows that they thought well enough of you to invest money in special training.[3]

You can do this by choosing several areas in which you're very skilled and claiming that you gained your expertise at special courses. Employers never check this out, as reference checking usually consists only of verifying college degrees and former employment. You must, however, have the skill to back up your statements. The worst mistake you can make, in this regard, is to state that you learned everything you know on the job. Lack of any academic background counts against you these days.

Yet another point is to be specific regarding dates of employment and separation. Simply listing the year isn't enough. One authority points out that, by listing only the year, what appears to be continuing employment may conceal a gap of up to a year. If you're going to list a job, list both year and month, and preferably the date, as well. This avoids leaving an obvious gap, and avoids giving the appearance of concealing information.[4]

## Applications

The next step in the employment screening process is the application form. In one sense, it's actually not very important, because all it does is present a framework for the interviewer to use in formulating questions. However, mistakes in filling out the application can be fatal to employment prospects! The reason is that many people admit too much, assuming that the prospective employer will find out all damaging information, anyway. This is a false assumption, as we'll see.

Fundamentally, you can provide any information you wish on an employment application. Follow your resume exactly when filling out the employment application. Remember that your resume and the application are the basic tools the interviewer will have, and that practically everything else he'll use or develop will come from information you provide him. Let's run over a few rules regarding employment applications, and how to build a good background for yourself:

1. Be prepared! This is the vital first step. You must have your story straight in your own mind, and be ready to deliver it in a convincing manner. With employment applications, the first step is to fill one out at your leisure, so that you

can massage the weak spots without being under a time limit. One way to do this is to pick up an application from a potential employer and ask if you can fill it out at home, as you have another appointment right then. Another way is to obtain employment application blanks from an office supply store. Yet another way is to apply for a job you don't want, and as soon as they hand you an application form, walk out with it. Make several photocopies as work sheets, and try several sets of answers to create the most credible background for yourself.

2. Do not provide any derogatory information in the employment application or any paperwork you fill out for any employer. NEVER! NEVER! NEVER! Do not admit to having been fired, using alcohol or drugs, or having any criminal convictions. If they want the dirt, let them dig for it! They usually don't, as we'll soon see.

3. When filling out any application or questionnaire, be realistic, and use common sense. This means not to try to "fake good" so much that you present an image of an angel or a "Dudley Do-right." It's all right to admit that you take an occasional drink. It's also permissible to know an alcoholic or two. You may even admit that you had an uncle who drank to excess. However, absolutely deny that you hang around with anyone who uses illegal drugs. You may admit having known such people in high school or college, because a denial would be incredible unless you attended a religious school. However, be careful to state that none of your current friends are dopers.

4. In some cases, you may need to cover a gap, such as a job from which you were fired, or time spent in prison or a psychiatric hospital. As a rule, the further in the past this gap is, the easier it will be to cover. One way is to list a totally fictitious job, with a company that no longer exists. If you have been working in the same field for some years,

you probably know of a real company that folded. The only problem you may have is encountering a former employee. The interviewer may tell you; "Come and meet Joe Blow. He used to work for the same company, and now works for us. You'll have a few things to talk over, I guess." In such a case, excuse yourself politely, and leave. You won't have much hope of faking your way through that unless you know something about the company and those who worked there. If you do, you may be able to bluff Joe Blow.

Another way to cover a gap is to claim employment out of state, or out of the country. Be careful, however, to have enough background to do this. If you claim you worked in Paris for two years, yet can't speak a word of French, you may meet someone who does. If you don't know the layout of the Paris subway, or the city's basic geography, and encounter an interviewer who does, you may be stuck for an answer if he asks you questions about Paris.

You may also claim to have worked for a relative. This is usually 100% secure, as an investigator often won't bother to ask a relative for any information. The best bet is a relative with a name different from yours, to mask the kinship. Your relative may even be willing to confirm your fictitious story.

Yet another way to cover a gap is to claim to have been hospitalized, or seriously disabled, for that period. If you have a limp, or other noticeable handicap, it's simple to list the time disabled to cover the questionable period. Remember to be precise with dates, to avoid suspicious questioning.

5. Faking higher education is also fairly easy, if you know what you're doing and the job requires a degree. You won't be able to fake a specialized education, if you're applying for a job as a biologist or machinist, without the

skill. However, claiming a bachelor's degree in liberal arts is a snap, if you're well-spoken. You may even be able to claim a master's degree, in some cases. Always make sure that your educational credits are from fairly well-known institutions.

## Background Checks

Although employers like to state or imply that every item of information on an application is subject to investigation, this is often only a ploy. Don't worry much about being unmasked by a background check. Many employers or employment interviewers are lazy or over-worked. It's surprising how many of them totally omit checking information which they could verify with a phone call.

Thorough background checks are also time-consuming and costly. Most employers omit them, or only spot-check their applicants. Some depend upon national investigating firms that specialize in providing background checks on employment applicants through their information networks. However, these companies deal in volume, and their background checks are superficial. This is why it's stupid to admit any damaging information at the outset.

Many applicants are worried sick that derogatory information will eventually come to light, and they confess all on their applications. Realistically, there's less chance of derogatory information coming out today than ever before, because of several lawsuits by former employees against employers who provided derogatory information to personnel investigators. Companies have had to pay damages because they impaired former employees' ability to obtain employment. This has chilled the atmosphere, and today hardly any employers will provide any information beyond verifying dates of employment, and possibly salary range.

The situation is so extreme that at least two nurses, suspected of killing ward patients, were able to find other employment because the hospitals for which they'd worked were afraid to badmouth them when prospective employers asked for references. Genene Jones, for example, had been suspected of killing patients in the pediatric intensive care ward of Bexar County Hospital, in San Antonio, Texas. She nevertheless was able to obtain employment with a Kerrville, Texas, pediatrician, because staffers at Bexar County Hospital kept quiet about their suspicions.

Another factor can work in your favor if you're thinking of leaving a job where you're having bad relations with your employer. In practically all cases, your employer would prefer that you leave voluntarily, rather than forcing him to fire you, because if you quit, his unemployment insurance premiums don't increase. It's also less troublesome to have an employee leave on good terms, rather than angry, because of the increasing numbers of reprisals taken by hostile former employees. Some commit sabotage before leaving. Others return to vandalize the property. One angry ex-employee returned to the printing company that had fired him in Louisville, Kentucky, and shot up the plant and personnel.

Some things are not subject to verification, because they lead to dead ends. Claiming employment with a defunct company leads an investigator to a dead end in most cases. Don't, however, list a totally fictitious company. Some investigative agencies keep back copies of telephone and city directories to check this out, because this trick has been used before.

Another important reason for giving only casual attention to the background check is the employer's or interviewer's ego. It should not be surprising that these people consider themselves experts on human nature, experts on "reading" and handling people, and experts at outwitting employees and employment applicants. After all, they're the successful power people, aren't they? If you're looking for a job, that makes you dependent on them, and places you in an inferior position, correct? Many employers make the mistake of thinking that, because someone who works for them is a subordinate, he's an inferior as well.

Let's look at a concrete example of how this works. Martin John Yate, author of one of the best books on interviewing and hiring practices today, lists eight reasons why some employers hire unsuitable people, including poor screening, poor interviewing, and poor questioning methods. Last on the list is failing to check references.[5]

Yate devotes most of his book to coaching the reader on how to spot inconsistencies and problem areas in a resume, and how to probe the applicant's personality with adroit questioning. The underlying theme is that the interviewer is smart enough to spot falsifications, and the applicant is not smart enough to outwit a conscientious interviewer. In the real world, this happens every day.

## The Interview

There are several types of interviewers you may face in your job hunt. One is the interviewer working for a state or private employment agency. These agencies are known colloquially as "body shops," because their main purpose is to move bodies. Their interviewers do the basic screening and send people who might be suitable to the employer. Such interviewers are often very low-quality people, especially those working for private agencies. Because they work on commission, they earn more money if they move more people. In their effort to refer people, they routinely misrepresent both the candidates and the employers.

You might feel gratified to hear such an interviewer describe you in glowing terms as he sets up an appointment for you with a prospective employer, but don't think for a minute that you've fooled him. He's just building up your image so that he can collect his commission.

You may be surprised to find that he's misrepresented the job to you in certain ways, such as citing a higher salary than it actually pays. If you ask him for an explanation, the standard reply is that the figure included benefits as well.

The other type of interviewer works for the company's personnel department. This person does the final screening, to ensure that only suitable candidates take up the supervisor's time.

The final person is the employer or supervisor himself. This is the person who makes the final decision regarding whom he'll hire. In small businesses the employer must be his own personnel department, and you don't face any intermediate interview.

Most professional employment interviewers aren't very bright. If they were, they wouldn't be holding down such poorly-paying jobs. They do, however, hold power over some of their fellow human beings, and they make the most of this. There are some who enjoy the power, and relish stomping on a person who is in a poor position to defend himself.

Most of this power is illusory. Personnel managers and interviewers are not the ones who make the final hiring decisions. As we've seen, they only do the preliminary screening. Still, in their role as gatekeepers, they have the power of first refusal, and they can make it hard on anyone who doesn't please them.

In this way, they're much like the arrogant telephone receptionist who insists on knowing what your call is about before she'll put you through. Occupying one of the low positions on the totem pole is frustrating, but some manage to take out their frustrations on people more helpless than they.

This is why many personnel people play mind games with their interviewees. They pretend to have special insights, attainable by using special psychological tricks, to select suitable people for their employers. Unfortunately, this intellectual masturbation doesn't serve any purpose but to confuse the entire process.

You may find the interviewer asking you a series of questions that appear meaningless, or unrelated to the job. Questions about your hobbies, for example, don't appear to be job-related at all, but some interviewers think that your hobbies reveal how social a person you are, and how well you get along with others.

Think about this if the sort of job you're seeking is one which requires public contact, or working with other employees. If an interviewer asks you what your hobbies are, don't say that you follow anything intellectual or that you can do alone, such as reading, or building model ships. Instead, mention bowling, playing cards, or any other activity that requires teamwork, or at least interaction with people. But if the job is a solitary one, such as monitoring gauges in a power plant, interpersonal relations aren't as important.

Keep in mind that many interviewers feel that a person's attitudes are guides to his or her behavior. If asked how you feel about people who steal from their employers, or who use illegal drugs, you must state that you strongly disapprove, and that you feel they ought to be punished. Any tolerance you show will lead the interviewer to suspect that you're either defending them because you're a druggie or a thief, or that you're on the verge of doing it.

Some interviewers are outright incompetent or lazy. This is the sort of interviewer that will ask you closed-ended questions, such as "Were you happy in your last job?" Only a fool would answer that he wasn't, because that would open the door to questions about how well he gets along with employers.

Here are some closed-ended questions that you should always answer with "yes," regardless of any skeptical manner the interviewer might adopt:

"Do you get along well with people?"

"Do you get along well with your supervisors?"

Here's a short list of closed-ended questions that require only a "no" answer, no matter how close to the truth they come:

"Were you ever arrested?"

"Were you ever fired?"

"Have you ever refused to obey your employer's orders?"

"Did you ever steal on the job?"

"Did you ever pass your company's proprietary information to unauthorized persons?"

"Do you use drugs?"

"Have you ever been to a psychiatrist?"

Another type of unskilled interviewer uses the ultimate open-ended question: "Tell me about yourself." The worst possible answer to this one is the question: "What would you like to know?" because it shows lack of poise. The proper answer is to describe your work experience, without quoting from your resume or application. Simply explain how you started in your field, and what you learned at each job. Tie it in with any special training for which your former employers paid.

You may encounter a skilled interviewer who uses "layered" questions. In asking about a specific area, he'll ask about different aspects of the same topic. For example, you might find him asking you these questions, in sequence:

"What was your main responsibility in your last job?"

"How did you handle it?"

"How many departments did you have to deal with in handling that?"

"What was the easiest part of handling that?"

"What was the most difficult aspect of handling that?"

"Did you have to work much overtime at it?"

Another layered sequence might relate to likes and dislikes:

"What did you like best about your last job?"

"What did you like the least?"

"Why?"

"How did you handle it?"

"Give me a specific example."

Layered questions are very probing, because a quick and superficial answer won't do. They're designed to expose the faker, and they work fairly well.

Another type of question you may hear is the negative or "stress" question. This is designed to force you to tell about your weaknesses. Some examples are:

"When was the last time you faced a problem you couldn't solve?"

"What duties do you like the least?"

"What do you find most difficult to do?"

"What is your weakest point?"

"What kind of decisions are hardest for you?"

"Why aren't you earning more?"

"What was it you disliked most about your boss?"

These test your poise, because you must answer them. You can't simply deny them all. You might state that you got along well with all of your supervisors, but you would not be able to make a credible case that you had always liked everything about every job you'd ever had.

The way to handle such questions is to put a positive spin on your answers. Reply that you don't like jobs in which you're not allowed to work to your full potential, that your weakest point is your impatience to get the job done, etc. The hardest decision for you should be which employees to lay off when the order comes down for a cut-back.

## Discriminatory Questions

It's illegal to ask questions relating to race, national origin, religious affiliation, political beliefs, etc. However, some employers still do, either directly or obliquely. This may not be offensive if you're the "right" religion, and this helps you get the job. If you're not, and you feel that the employer is discriminatory, you have to make a decision. Unfortunately, it's a decision that requires you to consider several aspects.

First, do you really want that job? Do you want to work for a person who would hold your religion or ethnic background against you?

Secondly, is the job so tempting that you'd want to sue or bring a complaint to the Equal Opportunity Employment Commission to get it? Would you be able to work in a place where you'd gotten the job through legal action?

Thirdly, is the effort worth the trouble, considering the time it will absorb? Can you afford to wait many months for a job, knowing that you might lose your case in the end?

When you consider all of these factors, you'll be able to decide whether you want to make an issue of discrimination, or to seek employment elsewhere.

## Rehearsing

The best way to learn which specific questions you're likely to face is to apply for jobs you don't really want. This will give you experience in interviewing, and practice in answering questions. You'll find it an enjoyable experience, because you won't have the nagging anxiety that often comes when your job depends on the results of the interview.

The other purpose that these dress rehearsals serve is to desensitize you. You'll get to feel more comfortable with practice, and when you go to interview for real, you'll feel more confident and at ease.

These dry runs also provide you with experience regarding employers in your area. You'll find out how closely they check references, for example. One way is to apply for several jobs entirely out of your field, and provide a totally faked employment history, to see how far you can go. You might get tripped up when an employer asks you specific job-related questions, but don't be surprised if one or more actually offers you a job.

Pre-employment interviews can appear intimidating, but in most cases they're not the free-for-alls that interviews with the media can be. Let's now examine the problems and pitfalls of talking to the press.

# Sources

1. *The Book of Lies,* M. Hirsch Goldberg, NY, William Morrow and Co., 1990, pp. 205-206.
2. *Hiring the Best,* Martin John Yate, Boston, MA, Bob Adams, Inc., 1988, p. 44.
3. *Ibid.,* p. 87.
4. *Ibid.,* p. 46.
5. *Ibid.,* p. 19.

# 12

# Media

# Interviews

Some people who have dealt with the media have horror stories to tell about being misquoted and unfairly treated. The reason is that some media people practice "advocacy journalism," slanting the news to support an evangelistic viewpoint. Others simply seek the most sensational aspect of a story to promote, in an effort to build their audience.

"Advocacy journalism" means that the reporter manages the news to push his or his editor's viewpoint. Selective reporting is a powerful tool, and is one way of slanting the news. In various forms, it's the foundation of advocacy journalism. You can't fight advocacy journalists, but you can avoid making their jobs easier.

Libel laws won't protect you if the media decide to do a number on you. There are ways of misrepresenting you that are above the law, and media people know all the tricks. The result is that you have to take steps to protect yourself. The first step is to understand why and how media people work, and the various stratagems they use to obtain damaging interviews.

## Giving Your Side of the Story

If you're involved in a controversy, or any type of litigation, a reporter may approach you with the stated purpose of giving you an opportunity to get "your side" across to the public. This is the same trick police use, and it's a cheap ploy to get you to talk. The reporter may even tease you with hints regarding what's allegedly been said about you. If you're suggestible, you may easily fall for this one.

## Biased Language

Some interviewers try to disparage you or your viewpoint by describing it in uncomplimentary terms. If you allow them to do this during an interview, you'll lose right at the outset.

Let's hypothesize that you're being interviewed after shooting someone who tried to hold you up on the subway. The reporter asks you: "How many vigilantes like yourself do you think are riding the subway?" If you let this slip by you, and allow the reporter to get away with labeling you a "vigilante," you'll put yourself in a bad light. The way to handle it is to tell the reporter forcefully: "I am not a vigilante. That's your term, not mine."

## Off The Record

At times, a reporter may ask you a question, set off by the phrase, "off the record." This purportedly means that he won't publish what you tell him, or attribute it to you. You accept such an assurance at your own risk. If you're a political candidate, and you believe a reporter's assurance that he'll treat your candid opinion of your opponent as "off the record," you may be surprised by a headline that states: "Smith Retarded, Says Jones."

Your statement might not make the headlines, but the reporter might use it as a lever to pry a statement from your opponent. This is especially true if you're being interviewed on camera. The reporter might also violate his promise to you, and run it in his news program.

Let's put this in capital letters, to burn it into your memory:

## NO INTERVIEW IS EVER OFF THE RECORD IF IT'S ON TAPE.

A TV interviewer might have the nerve to tell you that what you say to him is off the record, but as long as the camera's running, it's going on tape, and you might see it again on the six o'clock news. His promise to you, of course, will not be on tape.

The other side of this is that an unscrupulous reporter can use your off the record words to pry a statement out of your political opponent. Even without being involved in politics, your words can return to haunt you. An example is the reporter working on environmental or workplace hazards. If you blow the whistle on your employer, even off the record, you run the risk of having your words kick back in your face. If you divulge information known only to a few, and the reporter confronts your employer with it, it won't take much effort to figure out the source of the leak.

The best investigative reporters work very hard at protecting their sources, because they know it helps build their credibility. The only way to be sure of avoiding problems with statements made off the record is to speak only with well-known media people with track records of not "burning" their sources.

## The Ambush Interview

This is a favorite tactic among some pushy TV reporters. You emerge from your home or office to face a TV camera, and a reporter puts a microphone in front of your face and starts asking questions, without even introducing himself. If you get flustered, and say the first thing that comes into your mind, you'll probably say something you'll regret.

There's only one way to handle the ambush interview. Turn around and walk away. Don't acknowledge the reporter or the cameras. Don't say "No comment," because that produces a bad impression on TV. Don't even face the camera, once you see it, because that suggests you're cooperating in the interview. Simply turning your back, remaining silent, and totally ignoring all questions destroys the ambush interview, and sends the reporter down in flames.

## Remain Silent

The simplest way to avoid giving a reporter ammunition he can use against you is by keeping your mouth shut. "Silence Cannot Be Misquoted" is a good principle, and is the title of a book by the former press secretary of a politician who was savaged by the media during his career. It can be very hard to keep your mouth shut at times, because media people are very adept at persuading people to speak with them. Without police or subpoena powers, they cannot force you to talk, and they have to use guile instead of coercion.

In approaching you for an interview, a media representative may be very friendly and sympathetic. If you consent to the interview, you'll first hear a series of questions designed to get you off your guard. Near the end, you'll hear hostile questions.

A hostile question is one framed to put your actions, and your responses, in the worst possible light. This is the "Have you stopped beating your wife?" type of question that makes you appear guilty before you can answer. No matter how you answer it, you won't look good.

The only way to combat this type of treatment is to know with whom you are dealing. Never accept an invitation to an interview from an unknown. You and your press secretary can often tell, by scrutinizing the work of various media people, which ones are fair and which are merely seeking sensationalism. In fact, certain television interviewers have built reputations for hammering their interviewees, and these are the ones to avoid. A number of newspaper columnists are also noted distorters of fact, and their bias is obvious from reading their columns.

If in doubt, keep your mouth shut! This is especially important if you can't think on your feet. Remember, you're up against pros who know every verbal trick to elicit the information they want, and who know how to frame questions to control the answers. Unless you can match their skill, you're facing an unequal contest.

## The Final Cut

This is a TV term, and it signifies the final edited version of a program, the one which goes on the air. It's the electronic equivalent of editing, or selecting the material to present. The final cut is a powerful tool, because it allows a TV reporter, or his editor, to delete portions of an interview in which you look good, and include only those which show you hesitating, or saying "No comment."

One way to cope with this is to insist on control over the final cut yourself. This is a condition which few TV persons will accept, but it's an effective way to keep them from hammering you.

Media interviews can be harrowing, but you can fake them out. More difficult, however, is when you have to answer questions under oath. Sworn testimony is more intimidating, but it's also possible to handle it, as we'll see next.

# 13

# Depositions And

# Court Testimony

These are special situations, because every word you say goes on the official record. You're also under oath to tell the truth. Before we get into the nitty-gritty of sworn testimony, let's lay out a few points about attorneys:

1. Your attorney works for you, and you should be able to tell him everything relevant. You should be candid with him, because only if he knows the weak points of your case will he be able to forestall moves by the opposing attorney.

2. Your attorney's job is to represent you, and to get the best deal for you, whether the case is civil or criminal, and whether you're innocent or guilty. Guilty people are entitled to legal representation, too, under American law.

3. In a criminal case, you may be surprised to find your attorney not asking you if you're guilty. In some instances, he really doesn't want to know. His job is just to do the best he can for you, guilty or innocent.

4. In a criminal case, if your attorney is "Legal Aid Society" or otherwise court-appointed, don't expect too much. They're overworked, and they know that most of their clients are guilty, anyway. The most you may expect, as a rule, is that your attorney will try to cut the best "deal" he can with the prosecutor. You may be surprised to discover that at least 90% of criminal cases in this country include a "deal" in their dispositions.

There are all sorts of attorneys, in both civil and criminal fields. In civil practice, you will always want an attorney with you if you have to attend a deposition hearing. This is essential, because the attorney questioning you may try to bluff you into answering questions without legal justification.

## Depositions

These are question-and-answer sessions, under oath, during which you are obliged to answer the attorney's questions. You may have your attorney present, and he may object to improper questions, but a deft interrogator won't let this stop him.

The trick is "staying alive" during the question-and-answer session, and to present the appearance of truthfulness. At the moment, the only person you have to "sell" is the other side's attorney. If he thinks he's on to something, or that he can get you to reveal something you're trying to conceal, he'll come at you very forcefully. On the other hand, if he feels that you've been truthful, and that there's nothing to be gained from attacking, it will show in both his manner and the content of his questions.

The basic principle is the same as during interrogation: never give anything away.

Let's quickly review the basics of giving testimony, either in court or at a deposition hearing:

1. Look at your questioner, or at the jury.

2. Listen carefully to the questions, and think before answering.

3. Speak up, so that he, the judge and jury, and the court reporter can hear you.

4. Answer positively, without hedging.

5. If you don't know the answer, say so simply and directly.

6. Never change your testimony, or contradict anything you have said previously. This can be very important if you've previously made a written statement, and the attorney questioning you is going over the same ground. Never decide that you have a better answer now than before. Never assume that the attorney knows something to contradict your previous statement. Even a questioning look, raised eyebrow, or sidelong glance is totally insignificant, because it doesn't show in the court transcript.[1]

If you hesitate in responding, you can be sure that the attorney will notice this, and begin working around the question, asking you the same thing in a dozen different ways. If you don't answer the question, or if you hedge, he'll also take this as evasion. You can tell when he's zeroing in on the vital issue.

On the other hand, if the other attorney wastes time asking you routine questions about your address, where you lived before, your education, etc., he's simply marking time. He may try to ask you embarrassing questions, such as whether or not you've been to prison, confined in a psychiatric hospital, etc., but unless the answers are relevant to the issue, he's just trying to impress his client. Attorneys often use such posturing to convince their clients that they're earning their fees. You still have to be careful, though, because if you get caught in a lie on routine questions, you can be in for a hard time.

Note that the most important phrase is "get caught." Never assume that the other attorney knows more than he actually does. Don't assume that your previous statement wasn't good enough, and that you need to change it. Your statement may appear weak to you, or even have some obvious flaws, but only a contradiction is the kiss of death.

You can often get by with a weak case simply by repeating what you'd said previously. The other attorney may not pick up on the weak points. If you have a confident manner, you can "sell" yourself to a judge, jury, and even to your opponent's attorney.

This is why you've got to "sell" the other side's attorney the idea that you've got nothing to hide, or at least, that it's forever beyond his reach. A good analogy is a safe to which you're the only one who knows the combination, and he can't prove that you know it.

## Courtroom Testimony

The main differences between giving testimony at a deposition and in court are that court is more formal and structured, is larger, has more people present, and there's both direct examination and cross-examination. The attorney for the side for which you're testifying (remember, you may be a witness to a crime, civil action, etc.) will ask you questions about what you saw, heard, read, etc., to bring out the points he wishes. The opposing attorney has a chance to ask you questions of his own, to probe weak spots in your account and to open gaps in your testimony.

The direct examination is friendly questioning. Cross-examination is hostile, to break down or cast doubts upon your testimony. The attorney for your side should go over your testimony with you before your court appearance, and anticipate possible attacks from the other attorney. You ought to discuss these frankly with your attorney, and if there's anything you know that might adversely affect the case, bring it out before entering court. Don't leave any points as surprises to pop up during your testimony or cross-examination.

## Perjury

Perjury means lying under oath before an official body, or in special situations, such as deposition hearings. Perjury is a crime, and many prosecutors and attorneys use the threat of prosecution to coerce their subjects into providing the answers they want to hear. In reality, there are very few prosecutions for perjury, because it's truly a hard crime to prove, and few prosecutors try.[2]

Perjury is also often not worth prosecutorial effort, especially in domestic cases, such as divorce or custodial hearings. Everyone knows that in emotionally involved cases feelings run high, neither party is objective, and both parties shade the truth somewhat. It's simpler to overlook much of it, and allow a certain quota of lies.

For these reasons, perjury is often your best shot. The main points, when considering perjury, are how important the case is, and how can the other side prove that you knowingly lied. The other side may know that you're not telling the truth, but proving it is often hard to do.

If you're testifying in a case involving organized crime, there may be 50 investigators ready to run down evidence of perjury. If it's a divorce action, it's typically one party's word against the other's. Neither side has the people or the financial resources to devote to a massive effort.

If the perjury is a denial, the critical problem is what other evidence exists on the topic. If you're denying, for example, having written a certain check, there may be a check with your signature floating around out there, waiting for someone to scoop it up and introduce it as evidence. There may be one or more witnesses who saw you write it, who received it, or who saw someone else receive it. If any of these witnesses are close enough to find and bring to court, they may shoot down your testimony.

If faced with contradictory evidence, you can no longer stand by your story. In conceding, you have several ways out, although the other attorney, the judge, or the jury may not believe you. One is faulty memory. You might state that the incident took place so long ago, or was so insignificant, that you had forgotten it. This may work, in some cases, and save your credibility regarding other testimony.[3] However, you'll have lost that particular point, and opened the door to the other attorney's asking you if you're having another loss of memory regarding another point at issue.

The second way is to maintain that the question was unclear, or that you did not understand it. It can take some fast footwork, but you may be able to get away with it:

"Oh, you mean while I was living at home, before I moved out!"

"I thought you meant during my last job, not this one."

Contradictory evidence is not always there. This brings us back to self-contradiction. This is the only way in which you can do a number on yourself, and hand the adversary a victory on a platter. Keep your story "straight" and it won't happen.

# Sources

1. The author learned this lesson the hard way, but fortunately without paying a heavy price, during a deposition hearing relating to a divorce. The attorney was going over the answers to a questionnaire previously completed by the author, and at one point the author contradicted his written statement, thinking that the attorney might have had other information. Fortunately, this serious error was about a minor point that didn't surface again during litigation.

2. *The Book of Lies,* M. Hirsch Goldberg, NY, William Morrow and Co., 1990, pp. 34-35.

3. This can also kick back at you hard. One woman was faced with contradictory evidence regarding her date of birth, which she had falsely stated in a previous sworn statement. This led to several uncomfortable minutes during which she had several whispered conversations with her lawyer, but finally had to explain the discrepancy.

# Part III:

# Resistance

# 14

# Coping With

# Interrogation

We've covered various types of interrogations and interviews, and the range of tactics you're likely to encounter. It's now time to tie it all together, enabling you to design your plan to resist interrogation.

As we've seen, refusal to talk or answer questions is practical in only a few instances. When applying for employment, you cannot stand on your Fifth Amendment rights, for example. You therefore have to decide upon a basic stance, and a course of action, to guide you during the session. In a criminal investigation, you may decide that it's better to appear cooperative than to stonewall the investigation. Central to this is your personality.

# How Well Can You Resist?

As a start, examine your personality and behavior to form an appraisal of how well you might resist interrogation. Remember that interrogators like to see someone who is easy to manipulate, suggestible, and willing to talk. They probe for weaknesses to exploit. Nobody's perfect, and it's better to be aware of your weaknesses beforehand than to find them out during an interrogation, as a questioner takes you apart.

To find out your potential vulnerabilities, take this self-test to check out your weak spots. Think carefully about your answers, and be honest, because nobody will know but yourself. Answer the following questions about your behavior:

● Can you stand silence, when with another person, or do you feel a need to break the silence and say something?

If you can't stand silence, you're very vulnerable to an interrogator's staring at you, and making you uncomfortable enough that you start speaking.

● Are you very talkative?

If you are, it will work against you, unless you're an absolute chatterbox. Spilling every detail to an interrogator simply makes his job easier. However, if you constantly change subjects, interrupt yourself in mid-sentence, and return to ask him what he originally wanted, you can make it very hard for him to follow you, and you'll tire his mind quickly.

● Do you listen carefully when another speaks to you, or do you just wait for him to finish so that you can say something?

If you're eager to speak, you might find yourself blurting out something you later wish you hadn't said.

● Do you crave attention, or do you prefer people to ignore you?

If you crave attention, you'll be more receptive to an interrogator, especially if he "softens you up" first by leaving you alone in a room for hours.

● Do you contact your friends and acquaintances, as a rule, or do they call you?

This indicates whether you need people more than they need you, or vice versa. If you need human contact enough so that you're the one who initiates the contacts with friends and acquaintances, you're more vulnerable than you would be if people came to you. This is a dependency vulnerability.

● Are you suggestible? If someone tells you: "Look at that," do you immediately turn your head?

If you're very suggestible, this can work against you during interrogation, because the interrogator can exploit it to control your behavior. If he spots this weakness, he may take advantage of it by approaching you in a slow walk, flexing his muscles and scowling. Intellectually, you know that he's not going to attack you, but on a more basic and emotional level, this provokes fear.

Suggestibility also makes you more vulnerable to various deceptions employed by interrogators. Fake line-ups and identifications are more likely to prey on your mind.

● Do you snap out your answers to questions?

If you reply without thinking, you'll be especially vulnerable for two reasons. First, you won't be considering either the question or your answer carefully, and this leads to errors. The other reason is that sooner or later there will come a question that is truly probing, and you'll hesitate in answering. The interrogator will pick up on this, and know that he's hit upon a sensitive area.

● Do you often feel the need to explain and justify yourself?

If you do, you're very vulnerable to the interrogator who intimidates you with an accusing manner.

● Are you the "nervous" type, and do you show it by gestures and movements of the hands or feet?

As we saw several chapters ago, many interrogators believe that someone who blinks, looks at the ceiling, crosses his arms, etc., is deceptive. If you are normally fidgety, you'd better be aware of it, and understand the impression it makes on an interrogator. As we'll discuss later, you may want to practice appearing calm, or do relaxation exercises, in preparation for an interview or interrogation.

● How good is your resistance to pain?

You're not likely to be "worked over" in most situations, even in many foreign countries, but there are exceptions. In certain extreme situations, an interrogator may resort to force, and this can be very persuasive.

● Do you have a criminal record?

This is vital in determining how investigators treat you. A record is a very large black mark against you, if they know of it.

● What is your ethnic background?

To some, it will appear racist, but investigators go by common experience, which tells them that a Black man is more likely to be involved in street crime than a Caucasian. By the same token, if the crime is embezzlement, or stock fraud, they'll probably be looking for Caucasian suspects.

● What's your socio-economic level?

If you live in the ghetto, you're more likely to face abuse from investigators, because of the assumptions that you're uneducated and don't know your rights, and that you cannot afford a private attorney. Both police and private investigators know that legal-aid lawyers are too overworked to represent most of their clients properly, which gives investigators more latitude in their tactics.

## Avoiding Emotional Isolation

We've seen how police interrogators, by getting subjects away from familiar surroundings, or by taking advantage of a stressful situation, can break down a subject's resistance. Emotional isolation, being away from friends and relatives, can be devastating, and you should avoid it at all costs.

In practical terms, this means avoiding interrogations in unfamiliar surroundings, such as a police station. Many police investigators, even if they have no grounds for an arrest, prefer to invite a subject to their offices, where they can control the environment. They also like to separate the subject from his friends or relatives, or anyone else who might provide emotional support. Another reason, which they don't like to admit, is that they are lazy.

The basic rule for you to follow is that any questions they have for you may be asked on neutral ground, such as the sidewalk in front of your home. You should also try to have someone with you while answering police officers' questions. An attorney is best, but lacking an attorney, a close friend who is hard to intimidate is suitable.

A police officer will do his best to separate you from your friends or relatives. He may insinuate that anyone present is somehow an accomplice, or that he can start investigating them as well. This tactic may intimidate some people, but if you and your friends know your rights, you can cope with it.

If arrested, try to get a lawyer and bail as quickly as possible. Refuse to speak with police officers without a lawyer present. In this limited respect, you're in the driver's seat. The police have to be correct in their relationship with you. Failing to advise you of your rights, or failing to obtain the proper warrant if one is needed for a search, can throw their entire case out of court. By contrast, you don't have to be right. If you don't want to talk, they can't hold it against you in court.

Police and other investigators have little tricks to put their subjects at a disadvantage. One is to ask you: "What do your friends call you?" and then address you that way, in a false show of intimacy. The best reply to such a question is to ask: "Why do you want to know?"

## Cooperation

In some situations, it's better to appear to cooperate with police. This is when you're actually isolated, such as being stopped by an officer while you're alone. In such a case, it's best to answer his questions, and avoid antagonizing him in any way. The reason is that you're extremely vulnerable alone with a police officer, because whatever happens, it's your word against his. He may claim that you assaulted him, and that he had to subdue you. Unless you're 60 years old and infirm, you'll have trouble finding a judge to believe otherwise. Without witnesses, a court will probably accept his version of the events. If you end up under arrest anyway, wait until you see your attorney, and tell him what happened. In such a case, the claim that you confessed to avoid being beaten is worth presenting in court.

Also very relevant is your personal history. If you're a white-collar employee or a professional with a "clean" record, police will have a harder time making a jury believe that you were combative than if you're a vagrant with a record of violence.

## Presenting A Credible Front

It's not enough to plan to resist interrogation, because in many cases it's unavoidable. We're repeatedly facing questions about our backgrounds, employment records, daily work, and other mundane topics. This is why it's important to work hard on building a credible persona, a front that inspires confidence. Let's go over some factors that people use to judge the truthfulness of others. In so doing, let's keep in mind that the overall impression we present is as important, if not more so, than the response to a particular question. Professional confidence tricksters know this, which is why they work hard at presenting an appearance of respectability.[1]

### *Eye Contact*

Many sources, both authorities in the field and ordinary people, feel that maintaining eye contact is crucial. Failure to keep eye contact, or "shifty eyes," is a popularly accepted symptom of deception.[2] The most successful liars and con men know this, and cultivate a straightforward look, and will even stare into the other person's eyes.

Another aspect of eye contact is how people react to various types of questions. Try this on a wife or friend. Ask your helper to say his name or address. Watch the eyes, and note which way they move. Now ask him to multiply 11 times 12, and do a few other sums. Do his eyes move differently? Does the person stare up into the air, while calculating? Most peoples' eyes move differently when giving a response that requires thought or calculation instead of simply reciting from memory. This is supposedly a way of distinguishing invented answers from truthful ones.

The reasoning behind this theory falls down easily, when we think that many untruthful answers don't require much thought. The reply to the question, "Did you steal.......?" is simply "No."

A more complex reply, such as one explaining one's where-abouts during the time a crime took place, may require invention, but a clever liar will have his answer prepared and rehearsed.

Yet another theory is that the pupils dilate under stress, and this can betray a lie.[3] The problem with this theory is the same as the others: stress does not necessarily denote a lie. However, if someone thinks you're lying because he sees your pupils dilate, it's still trouble for you.

### Speech

There have been controlled experiments regarding how speech patterns change when someone is lying. Allegedly, a person lying slows down, and the pitch of his voice rises. There's also an increase in slips of the tongue, and an increase in bridging sounds, such as "um" and "uh."[4] This, again, shows an increase in anxiety and stress, but not necessarily untruthfulness. Controlled experiments are not parallel to actual conditions, such as a person's trying to avert suspicion of a crime.

Liars also allegedly force smiles when they lie. This is some-times obvious, especially when there's an evident pattern of de-ception, but it also is a symptom of embarrassment. Sweating is also a sign of emotional stress, which some interrogators inter-pret as proof of deception. Both can mean simple nervousness. Common experience shows this very clearly.

### Disarming Candor

A poor tactic is to try to "fake good" about everything. No-body's perfect, and many interviewers test their subjects' truthfulness by questioning them about personal faults, such as whether they were ever late to work, or ever took home any company property. While it's wise to deny having been fired, or having a criminal record, it's pointless and stupid to deny minor faults. Most successful interviewees understand this intuitively, and adopt a pose of disarming frankness. This means cheerfully admitting to having made small mistakes, giving an impression of candor. Let's look at one way to handle a question, using disarming candor:

"Have you ever been late for work?"

"Yes, once I forgot to set the alarm, and I was two hours late. My boss was very nice about it, and didn't chew me out. I felt so badly about it that I made sure I was never late again."

This makes several points. First, it shows "honesty" in admitting a misdeed. Secondly, it portrays good relations with a former supervisor. Thirdly, it shows that the subject learned from his mistake.

Don't go overboard in admitting faults. It's allowable to admit small errors and various character traits, but a major error to admit to anything serious. This is especially true if you're being interrogated on a criminal matter.

Never admit to a criminal record of any sort. Many investigators are lazy, as are civilian interviewers, and prefer to have their suspects do their work for them. Admitting to having been arrested or convicted simply leads to more incriminating disclosures. Your chances of concealing a record are not as bad as many think. First, the National Crime Information System is glutted with records, and contains a percentage of errors and omissions that is a closely guarded secret. Your record might simply have gotten lost. Your chances are even better if your conviction was in another state. The record will be only in the NCIC, and not in your present state's computerized memory. If your record is very old, it might never have been entered into any computer.

Some investigators are thorough, and some are simply lucky. A check might turn up a conviction, and the investigator may use this against you, accusing you of lying to him. Your comeback is simply that you were innocent. You didn't mention it because, despite the conviction, you didn't actually do it. If the investigator insists that you were guilty, reply that your conviction was overturned on appeal. He's not likely to check this out, unless you're under suspicion of a very serious crime.

Finally, don't contradict yourself. This is so crucial that you must take extra steps to ensure that it doesn't happen. Run over your statement in your mind before appearing for any interrogation or interview. This is easy to do when seeking employment, because you have ample time to compose and review your resume, and fill out employment applications. In a criminal setting, you may not have the time, and you'll have to think on your feet and keep it simple. This is true whether you're guilty or innocent.

Police investigators, attorneys, and other interrogators know that showing a subject a contradiction in his statements is often a pry-bar to "breaking" his story. This is why they question suspects for hours, going over the same ground again and again, until the tired suspect makes a mistake and contradicts himself.

There are several ways to cope with this tactic:

1. Tell the interrogator that you're tired, and want to stop.

2. State that you won't make any statements without your attorney being present. Your attorney will coach you, and help you cope with the questions.

3. Purposely misstate several answers, to show the interrogator that he's not going to get any more useful information from you. Make sure that your misstatements are not about critical facts, though.

### *Assertiveness*

You also need to be assertive, without being offensive. This is walking a fine line between sticking up for yourself, so that an interviewer can't bulldoze you, and being too aggressive, so that he feels that you "come on too strong." You have to show poise.

Always remember that some people are power-oriented, and see relationships only in terms of power politics and intimidation. In an interview, they'll test you to see if they can push you around.

The main rule is to be polite, both in manner and choice of words. You'll find this balance necessary to counter some verbal tricks interviewers use. Let's get into the nitty-gritty of using assertiveness to avoid being bulldozed.

Some interviewers like trick questions, loaded questions, and other subtle and unsubtle manipulative techniques. Some like word games because of the feeling of power they get from using them, while others feel that dishonest questioning has tactical value.

An example of a dishonest question is the "predicated question," or "leading question," asking something based on an assumption, in the expectation of forcing an admission. Psychologists love to use this trick, when they ask: "At what age did you first masturbate?" An employment interviewer may use a variation on this theme by asking:

"When were you last fired?"

"Tell me about the last argument you had with a supervisor."

This is where you have to calmly and politely contradict the interviewer, and explain that you've never been fired, or that you never argue with a supervisor.

A situation demanding quick assertiveness is the silence following a feedback statement. The interviewer will repeat a word, phrase, or sentence from your last statement, and sit and stare at you, as if expecting an answer. If you've just told him that you managed a prototype program in your last job, he may repeat "Prototype?" and look at you.

If this happens, there are two ways of handling it.

The first is to nod and say, "Yes, prototype."

If he refuses to move on to another question, and continues to stare, give him a few more seconds, to be polite. Then ask him: "Do you have any other questions?" as if the interview may close right then. Another way is to ask: "Can I ask you some questions?" If he agrees, you then pose questions about the company, its benefits, etc. This is the polite way of regaining control of the interview. If he wants more information, he'll have to ask you for it.

Some interviewers try to hit you with reflexive questions, making a statement followed by "Don't you agree?" The way to handle this, if you don't agree, is to tell him that you're not sure of his meaning, and ask him to explain further.

A reflexive question may be designed to suggest the answer, but for a devious purpose. The interviewer may be probing for the applicant's views, and testing his sincerity at the same time. It's a sort of test, loaded against the applicant, because to give the right answer, he has to buck the interviewer. Coping with this may appear tricky, but the technique is actually very straight-forward. Let's look at an example:

Q: "We think that telephone follow-up should begin within ten days of after we place an order, don't you?"

This is one of those maybe questions, because the answer could go either way. The safe course is not to contradict the interviewer, but show him that there's another way, and express your willingness to do things his way, if he wishes. Here's how you might answer him:

"Where I worked before, my supervisor had me always send out a follow-up letter, and I only phoned if the vendor didn't answer the letter promptly. What procedure would you like me to follow here?"

This answer doesn't contradict him directly. Instead, it shows that you followed another procedure because it was standard at your previous job.

Some interviewers are addicted to "stress interviewing," which is a technique of keeping the subject off-balance with tough questions. This has some justification if the object is to test the subject for ability to stand up under pressure relevant to the job. An applicant for a media or public relations job may have to be able to think on his feet, and retain his poise in difficult situations.[5]

This can backfire, however, by antagonizing the candidate. One qualified individual took such offense at the way he was treated that he stated emphatically that he would never work for that person.[6]

### Body Language

Hand movement also supposedly betrays the liar. The person whose hands move a lot, especially if rubbing the face, is supposedly a liar. Unfortunately, this, too, is uncertain. There are cultural variations in hand movements.[7]

The major problem is that many interrogators accept certain types of behavior as symptoms of deception. Some authorities even list these symptoms for their disciples to read.[8] If you encounter one of these, and you happen to be the nervous type, you'll appear deceptive to him.

You can, however, correct some of these behavior patterns. A basic step is to learn to practice relaxation exercises. You can use these before interrogation, and even during the session. If it's a criminal interrogation, you can be quite open about it. When the interrogator sees you squirming, tell him forthrightly that you're doing relaxation exercises because you've never been a criminal suspect before.[9]

## *Preparation*

In most cases, you'll have ample time to prepare for the session. If you're job-hunting, have a friend ask you likely questions before you go for an interview. While it's not possible to anticipate every question an interviewer might throw at you, you can get an idea of which questions are in vogue in your area.[10] Simply go for a few dry runs, applying for jobs you don't really want, to gain exposure to current interviewing practice.

Rehearse your answers. Go over the questions you think an interviewer will pose, and try different answers to each, so that your friend can form an opinion regarding how well they come across to him. Rehearsing your answers will also produce "desensitization" to any anxiety that the topics may produce. Your blood pressure may, for example, jump at the question: "Have you ever been fired?" or "Have you ever stolen anything?" After practicing saying "No" or "Never" a few dozen times, you'll find yourself calming down.

When rehearsing your answers, don't try to polish them word-for-word. Interviewers may pick up on answers that seem too pat, and this can alert them to something wrong.

Another point to watch, both when formulating your answers and when responding to surprise questions, is to give a direct answer, if you can. Never evade or equivocate. If an interviewer asks you if you've ever been convicted of a felony, never answer the question with a question, such as "A real felony?" or ask him to repeat the question. Never say, "No, not really," as this sounds weak. Simply say, "No." If he asks a question to which you don't know the reply, simply say, "I don't know."

This point is critically important. Direct answers always present a more confident front than any sort of qualified answer. Saying: "I suppose so," or "I'm not that sort of person," sounds weaseling, and even a bored or stupid interrogator will quickly pick up on this. If you can answer a question with a "yes" or "no," do so.

The best policy is to provide short answers, just long enough to answer the question adequately. It's not necessary to explain, if a simple "yes" or "no" will do. In fact, volunteering information can often sound defensive, and defensiveness implies that there is something which needs defending.

## Tactical Resistance

Just as there are tactical systems in interrogation, there are systems for resisting. Unless you refuse outright to talk, you'll have to hold a dialogue with your accusers.

Resistance can be total or partial. Total resistance is simply refusing to discuss the case at all. It's all right to ask for food, water, and other amenities.

The first, and simplest, step is outright denial. Deny, deny, deny, and claim that they've got the wrong suspect. This isn't too bad a tactic to use, because interrogators expect it. If you cave in and tell all right away, they may think that you're trying to con them, and they'll continue probing to uncover the "truth."

One way to counter an interrogator's appeals is to shake your head "no" whenever he begins to speak. This non-verbal language makes it clear that you're totally rejecting everything he's trying to tell you. Even the most verbally skilled interrogators can't defeat this tactic by words alone. An unskilled interrogator will lose his poise if you use this tactic against him.

Another way is to appear confused. Contradict yourself on innocuous points, to create doubt in the interrogator's mind regarding your reliability as an informant.

## Exploiting Interrogators' Mistakes

The fundamental point here is to be familiar with interrogation tricks and tactics, and to be ready to use them against the interrogator when you can. If you're familiar with the various tactics, both straightforward and deceptive, that interrogators use, you have a road map of the interview. When you notice the interrogator begin one of the standard tricks, you can prepare a counter-move. Sometimes, it pays to refuse to respond to a trick. In other cases, it may be helpful to pretend to be fooled.

The "good guy-bad guy" trick, with one interrogator harsh and demanding and the other pleasant, is very old, but it still works with some people. You may choose to counter it by treating both the good guy and the bad guy alike. You may also seek to exploit this trick in your favor. The technique is to appeal to the good guy when the bad guy leaves the room. You might say something like this:

"Look, I really didn't do it, but how am I going to convince him of that? He's just out to get me."

Another point is to try to glean information from what the interrogator asks. Listen carefully to every word of every question. The reason is that questions themselves often give you clues regarding what your interrogators already know. If, for example, you're asked, "On what day did you go to the empty warehouse to hide the money?" the question reveals that they know about both the empty warehouse and the money.

Poorly-trained, unskilled, or over-confident interrogators often say more than they should, giving away information to their subjects. This is how they contaminate an interrogation. It's bad to blab, whether you're on one side of the fence or the other. Try to build a picture of what they know, and what they don't know, so that you can limit yourself to admitting only what they already know.

# Advance Preparation

Prepare as many answers in advance as you can. This will give you a more confident manner than if you have to invent answers on the spur of the moment. If you're trying to describe a person or place, don't try to invent someone or some place with which you're totally unfamiliar. If you state that you saw someone running away when you found a dead body, describe someone you know well instead of inventing a description. Remember that you may have to repeat your description several times, and that you must be fairly consistent.[11] The exception to this, of course, is if an event took place in light too poor to allow a good view of the person.

If you're presenting an alibi, be sure of your details. For example, if you say that you were at a movie at a certain time, be prepared to state the title of the film and to provide a synopsis of its plot. It's safe to expect that they'll check. Likewise if you claim to have been in another city at a critical time. Don't mention a city you've never seen, because you can expect to be asked where you stayed, where you took meals, and other questions to test your familiarity with the locale.

The back-up story is always a possibility if your story breaks down. This is a common and well-known trick used by spies and professional criminals, but it still works, as does the "good guy-bad guy" ploy interrogators use. To avoid confessing to what you really need to hide, you tell a story against yourself. If you have to explain your presence in a certain restaurant, you can say that you were meeting a married woman. The sleazier the circumstances, and the worse light they cast on you, the easier it will be to get the story believed. This is especially true if your interrogator has a dirty mind and a taste for raunch. A good whips-and-chains story may convince him, and distract him from pursuing the real issue. If you really want to get raunchy, you can say that you were involved in a homosexual pick-up. It beats confessing to murder.

# Don'ts

Don't volunteer information. If you can answer a question with a "yes" or "no," do it, and don't add anything unless asked. Always remember that supplying additional information leads only to more questions. If the interrogator wants to know something, let him ask about it directly. Make him work for his money.

Don't display a sullen silence, unless you've refused to talk until your attorney arrives. An interrogator will interpret silence as a way of concealing something, and will hold it against you.

Don't adopt a super-calm manner, devoid of emotion. An "iceberg" manner turns people off, and provokes resentment. It's also not normal, because people react and show emotion in certain situations. If your questioner is a psychologist or psychiatrist, he'll interpret an iceberg manner as "flattening of affect," which is a symptom of schizophrenia. Remember, an appropriate emotional response always works in your favor, not against you.

Don't allow the interrogator to feel, by your manner or by your statements, that you think yourself smarter than he is, or that you look down upon him. You'll antagonize him, and he'll only cause you problems later. A superior attitude can win the battle, but lose the war.

Don't be flip during questioning. This can easily give the impression that you don't take the business seriously, and antagonize your questioner. The personal equation is very important, and if your interviewer feels that you don't show proper respect, he'll resent it.

Don't play smart-ass, to an interrogator or to anyone else in an official capacity. You may be tempted to do this, if your attorney gets you bail and frees you from police custody, but resist the temptation. If you antagonize a police officer or a private investigator, you'll make it a personal matter, and he'll remember you. Much later, he may get an opportunity for "payback."

Don't shoot your mouth off, either to an interrogator or to someone whom you consider a "friend." Remember that one of the investigator's most useful tools is the informer, and that the person to whom you are revealing damaging information may be itching to run to the interrogator to repeat what you tell him. Always remember the "need to know" principle.

This last point is crucial, because there's an emotional letdown after an interrogation is over. We've already seen how some interviewers use this period to induce a subject to drop his guard. If you relax while still in the interrogator's presence, or with someone whom you falsely think is on your side, you may reveal something inadvertently.

# Sources

1. *The Rip-off Book,* Victor Santoro, Port Townsend, WA, Loompanics Unlimited, 1984, p. 21.

2. *The Book of Lies,* M. Hirsch Goldberg, NY, William Morrow and Co., 1990, pp. 233-234.

3. *Ibid.,* p. 234. Also *Law and Order,* August, 1990, p. 95.

4. *Ibid.,* pp. 234-235.

5. *Hiring the Best,* Martin John Yate, Boston, MA, Bob Adams, Inc., 1988, p. 74.

6. *Ibid.,* p. 74.

7. *Telling Lies,* Paul Ekman, NY, W. W. Norton Co., 1985, pp. 105-109.

8. *Criminal Interrogation,* Arthur S. Aubry and Rudolph R. Caputo, Springfield, IL, Charles C. Thomas, Publisher, 1980, pp. 244-255.

9. *Interrogation,* Burt Rapp, Port Townsend, WA, Loompanics Unlimited, 1984, p. 214.

10. Personnel interviewing is a trendy art. Simply asking job-related questions is old-fashioned, and modern interviewers try to be clever, following whichever theory is fashionable at the moment.

11. *A Handbook For Spies,* Wolfgang Lotz, NY, Harper & Row, 1980, p. 122.

# 15

# The Language

# Of Lies

A relatively new field in the behavioral sciences is linguistics, the study of the use of language, and the hidden meanings in choice of words. This has application in general and clinical psychology, and in criminal investigation.

Studying the language of a statement can disclose a person's educational level, familiarity with the language, possible foreign origin, and in certain cases, signs of mental disorder. Scrutinizing the structure and content of a statement can also provide clues to deception.

The theory is that the way a person expresses himself gives indications of truthfulness or deception. This is so obvious that it needs no scientific proof. A person who answers a question with a question is evidently evading the question. So is one who deflects the question by giving an inappropriate answer. Others hedge their answers, or claim not to remember the facts in question. These behaviors are cross-cultural, and do not depend upon a particular language or even level of education. An educated person will, obviously, be able to compose his answers in more sophisticated language, but the same purpose and principles apply.

## Tactics of Deception

Most people are fairly truthful, in the sense that they won't tell an outright lie. Instead, they'll provide answers in weaseling language, glossing over relevant facts, and withholding relevant information. The reason is that they want to avoid committing themselves to an untruth.

Both structure and content are important. For example, the use of pronouns often discloses something about the relationship when describing the actions of two or more persons. A clerk describing a stick-up, for example, is more likely to say: "The gunman took me into the back room," or "He took me into the back room," than "We went to the back room." Using separate pronouns reinforces that the clerk and the gunman are not allies, but adversaries. "We" would be inappropriate in this case, because it would imply that they acted in conjunction.

A change in the use of pronouns in a statement indicates a change in the relationship. It sometimes happens that a victim begins actively cooperating with a captor. It can also indicate a period of emotional stress. A victim's statement might begin with:

"He came in and pulled a gun from his pocket. He said it was a stick-up, and I raised my hands. He moved over to the cash register."

In discussing his feelings during the episode, the victim may well shift pronouns:

"When something like this happens, you feel it's not really happening to you. You see things in a daze, and nothing seems real."

There may be gaps in the narrative, which the subject fills by phrases such as "afterwards" to bridge time, and "We talked," without indicating what the conversation contained. These are indications for further questioning.

A statement's contents can also provide clues to deception. A general rule is that the person who experienced something experienced the entire event, not only the details important to the investigation. The net result is that a truthful statement will be rich in details, while a false one will be a stripped-down version, lacking details that verify the statement.

A fabricated story tends to be more straight-forward and logical than a truthful one. The statement often shows better emotional control than would be logical to expect, and relates the incidents in a manner that leads to a logical conclusion. Real life is rarely this neat.

## Practiced Liars

Some people enjoy deception. These belong to the minority we call "pathological liars." They won't tell the truth without embellishment, or distortion, even when it serves no purpose. These are the types of people who gravitate into certain occupations, such as sales, advertising, public relations, or politics.

They intuitively know that the best way to put across a lie is to tell it forcefully and boldly. They know the "big lie" technique by heart, and practice it. They won't trip themselves up by weak statements, or playing word games.

These people are very hard to catch in a lie, without outside information. They can look straight in your eye and lie to you, without hesitation and without anxiety. Unless you know, from independently developed information, that their statements are false, you can't tell that they're lying.

# Deception

We can learn from the successes of professional liars, and from the errors of those who try to lie, but fail. The main point is to state a lie boldly and confidently, without hesitation and without hedging.

# Glossary

**Big Lie**   The technique of telling a lie so bold that it fools the listener because he can't imagine that someone would lie about something so important or basic. The liar may claim to be a doctor, or a millionaire, both of which are easy to check. The victim does not check, because he feels it would be unnecessary.

**Closed-ended Question**   A question allowing only a "yes" or "no" answer, or a very short answer. Examples are: "Were you ever fired?" "Where do you live?"

**Confession**   Admitting to an act. A confession may be true or false. False confessions come about as a result of coercion, or a mental quirk by the confessor. Some people have an urge to confess to sensational crimes, appearing at police stations to surrender. Others confess under pressure, because of fatigue or simply to stop the discomfort.

***Cop-out*** Slang for a plea bargain.

***Copping the Plea*** Same as "cop-out."

***Deal*** Catch-all term for any agreement for special consideration with an investigator or a prosecutor. This may be a plea-bargain, or an exchange of information for special treatment.

***Faking Good*** Falsification of credentials or answers to make oneself appear better than the facts justify. This term is often employed by people who administer polygraph tests, honesty questionnaires, etc.

***Feeding Back*** An interviewer's repeating a sentence or phrase that the subject has just uttered, and looking at him expectantly, to elicit more details. This is also known as the "mirror" technique.

***"Good Guy-Bad Guy"*** A form of role-playing by a pair of interrogators, in which they whipsaw the suspect by alternating harsh with kind treatment. One interrogator plays the "bad guy," snarling at the suspect and threatening him with dire consequences if he doesn't cooperate. The other provides emotional relief by being kind and considerate, and tactfully asking the suspect to get what he knows off his chest.

***Informant*** Anyone who can provide information to an investigator or police officer. An informant may be a witness to a crime, a victim, or anyone else who has any sort of useful information.

***Informer*** A suspect or convicted criminal who provides information to an investigator in return for special consideration. In practice, many informers volunteer for the task, preferring to inform on a friend or associate than face a criminal charge alone.

***Interrogation***   Questioning of a suspect during a criminal investigation.

***Interview***   Questioning in a non-criminal setting, or of people who are not suspects, e.g., witnesses.

***Investigative Key***   A fact about a crime, which the investigator keeps to himself, as an authenticator in case of a confession. An example might be the type of knife used, something which only someone at the scene would know.

***Leading Question***   Same as "Predicated Question."

***Lie Detector***   Common term for "polygraph."

***Mirandize***   To give a suspect the "Miranda Warning" when placing him under arrest or before beginning a custodial interrogation.

***Official Police***   Police agents working for local, state, or the federal government.

***Open-ended Question***   A type of question designed to give the interviewee the maximum latitude in answering. One such question is: "Tell me about yourself."

***Plea Bargain***   A deal, worked out between the prosecutor and the defendant's attorney, for a reduced charge or sentence in exchange for a guilty plea.

***Police***   We use this term only for police agents of state or local government, and for federal agents. Privately employed officers are "security guards" or "security agents."

***Polygraph***   An instrument to measure and record heart rate, blood pressure, breathing, and skin conductivity, as stress indicators.

***Predicated Question***   A question based upon an assumption, which tends to force a certain type of answer. One such question is: "When were you last fired?"

***Pressure***   Verbal techniques of making the interviewee uncomfortable or anxious. Also includes techniques which have physical effects, such as withholding food, water, tobacco, or permission to go to the toilet.

***Private Security Guard***   A person performing security or guard work for a private agency, unconnected with any government.

***Roll Over***   Slang term for cooperating with the investigator. A suspect may "roll over" on his partner, providing testimony in return for a lesser sentence.

***Salami Slicing***   Enticing admissions from a subject in small increments.

***Security Guard***   Same as "Private Security Guard."

***Stonewalling***   Outright refusal to cooperate. This can take the form of repeated denials, refusal to be interviewed or make any statement, and refusal to answer any questions, even apparently unrelated ones.

***Subject***   A person being interviewed, or under interrogation, who is not necessarily suspected of a crime.

***Suspect***   Any person suspected of having committed, or taken part in, a crime.

***Telephone***   A slang term for an electric-shock machine used for torture. Originally, this was literally a field telephone, with a hand-cranked magneto, used to produce the high-voltage current for eliciting confessions. Today, there are sophisticated plug-in devices built into briefcases, that allow setting the voltage desired, and with an array of clamps and electrodes to fit any part of the body.

***Torture***   Physical techniques of making the interviewee uncomfortable or anxious.

**Truth Drug**   Also known as "Truth serum." Drugs which break down inhibitions and supposedly bring out the truth. Information elicited this way is unreliable, because subjects are suggestible.

**Turn Over**   Same as "roll over."

**Voice Stress Analyzer**   An electronic device to measure and record voice pitch and undertones. This is as unreliable as the polygraph.

# For Further

# Reading

***The Book of Lies,*** M. Hirsch Goldberg, NY, William Morrow and Co., 1990. This is an entertaining, anecdotal book, with a serious underlying tone. It puts the problem of resisting interrogation into perspective, and provides practical pointers on both detecting and practicing deception.

***Elementary Field Interrogation,*** Dirk von Schrader, El Dorado, AR, Delta Press, 1978. This is a textbook of torture, with some attention given to psychological preparation.

***A Handbook For Spies,*** Wolfgang Lotz, NY, Harper & Row, 1980. Wolfgang Lotz has "been there," because he's been arrested and interrogated in Egypt as a spy for Israel. He had the luck to survive the experience because he was able to pass for German instead of Jewish, and is therefore able to tell what it's like to get the full treatment by the secret police.

***Hiring the Best,*** Martin John Yate, Boston, MA, Bob Adams, Inc., 1988. This is probably the best book on pre-employment interviewing written in America, because it's clear, logical, and complete. Its main value is its focus on the tactics of interviewing, providing practical advice instead of abstruse principles. This book, is, however, misleading in one important aspect. Few employers can afford to hire the "best," and have to be satisfied with those who are willing to work for what they're willing to pay. This is why you're unlikely to find yourself confronted with the slick interviewing techniques explained in this book.

***Interrogation,*** Burt Rapp, Port Townsend, WA, Loompanics Unlimited, 1987. This provides the full picture from the other side of the hill. This manual covers all aspects of interrogation and interviewing, including physical coercion, techno-tactics, personality tests, and other means.

***Knock 'em Dead,*** John Martin Yate, Boston, MA, Bob Adams, Inc., 1987. This book is the mirror image of *Hiring the Best,* cited above, because it's a guide to interviewing from the applicant's point of view. This volume contains Yate's recommended answers to various tough questions and trick questions hiring interviewers are likely to ask.

***Lie Detection Manual,*** Dr. Harold Feldman, Belleville, NJ, Law Enforcement Associates, 1982. This is a standard polygraph manual, which provides the rationale behind the tests, the structuring of questions, and interpretation of the answers. This book gives a good insight into the mind-set of the polygraph "expert," which is useful in coping with a polygraph test.

*Notable Crime Investigations,* William Bryan Anderson, Editor, Springfield, IL, Charles C. Thomas, Publisher, 1987. This book contains some insights into the techniques of police interrogation. Each chapter is a narrative, and the editor summarizes some investigative tips for the reader at the end.

*The Mugging,* Morton Hunt, NY, Signet Books, 1972. This book is a detailed account of a mugging in New York, and its aftermath. Its value is the meticulous way it explains how the criminal justice system works, although few systems are as badly overloaded and out of date as New York City's. Pages 95-136 contain a good narrative of the interrogation, as practiced by the hard-boiled New York City detectives assigned to the case.

*The Spy Who Got Away,* David Wise, NY, Avon Books, 1988. The value of this book is in the detailed description of how the FBI treated Mrs. Howard after her husband defected to Russia. This is an explicit account of how emotional isolation can lead to revealing secrets, if the manipulators are at all clever about it.

# Index

# You Will Also Want To Read:

☐ **58047 INTERROGATION: A Complete Handbook,** *by Burt Rapp.* A complete manual on interrogation includes: The history of interrogation, The basics of effective interrogation, Examination and cross-examination, Why interrogations sometimes fail, And much more. Everything you ever wanted to know about interrogation, but were afraid to ask! *1987, 5½ x 8½, 230 pp, soft cover.* $14.95

☐ **88114 HOW TO BEAT "HONESTY" TESTS,** *by Sneaky Pete.* This book takes a close look at these tests. Most honesty tests are provided by three companies, and they have predictable patterns. This book will show you how they work and how to defeat their attempts to probe your psyche. *1989, 5½ x 8½, 46 pp, soft cover.* $5.95

☐ **76041 THE OUTLAW'S BIBLE,** *by E.X. Boozhie.* This is a real life civics lesson for citizen lawbreakers: how to dance on the fine line between freedom and incarceration, how to tiptoe the tightrope of due process. Covers detention, interrogation, searches and seizures. The only non-violent weapon available for those on the wrong side of the law. *1985, 5½ x 8½, 336 pp, index, soft cover.* $14.95

☐ **19079 FIGHTING BACK ON THE JOB,** *by Victor Santoro.* One of the most satisfying "revenge" books ever published! Tells how to strike back against a lousy boss, jerk fellow employees, the company spy, and anyone else in the workplace who has ticked you off. *Sold for entertainment purposes only. 1982, 5½ x 8½, 149 pp, illustrated, soft cover.* $10.00

*And much more! We offer the very finest in controversial and unusual books — please turn to our catalog announcement on the next page.*

_____**NQ1**

**Loompanics Unlimited/PO Box 1197/Port Townsend, WA 98368**

Please send me the titles I have checked above. I have enclosed $ _____ (including $3.00 for shipping and handling of 1 to 3 books, $6.00 for 4 or more).

Name _____

Address _____

City/State/Zip _____

*(Washington residents include 7.8% sales tax.)*

*"Yes, there are books about the skills of apocalypse — spying, surveillance, fraud, wiretapping, smuggling, self-defense, lockpicking, gunmanship, eavesdropping, car chasing, civil warfare, surviving jail, and dropping out of sight. Apparently writing books is the way mercenaries bring in spare cash between wars. The books are useful, and it's good the information is freely available (and they definitely inspire interesting dreams), but their advice should be taken with a salt shaker or two and all your wits. A few of these volumes are truly scary. Loompanics is the best of the Libertarian suppliers who carry them. Though full of 'you'll-wish-you'd-read-these-when-it's-too-late' rhetoric, their catalog is genuinely informative."*

— **THE NEXT WHOLE EARTH CATALOG**

# THE BEST BOOK CATALOG IN THE WORLD!!!

We offer hard-to-find books on the world's most unusual subjects. Here are a few of the topics covered IN DEPTH in our exciting new catalog:

- *Hiding/concealment of physical objects! A complete section of the best books ever written on hiding things!*

- *Fake ID/Alternate Identities! The most comprehensive selection of books on this little-known subject ever offered for sale! You have to see it to believe it!*

- *Investigative/Undercover methods and techniques! Professional secrets known only to a few, now revealed to you to use! Actual police manuals on shadowing and surveillance!*

- *And much, much more, including Locks and Locksmithing, Self-Defense, Intelligence Increase, Life Extension, Money-Making Opportunities, and more!*

Our book catalog is 8½ x 11, packed with over 700 of the most controversial and unusual books ever printed! You can order every book listed! Periodic supplements to keep you posted on the LATEST titles available!!! Our catalog is free with the order of any book on the previous page — or is $3.00 if ordered by itself.

*Our book catalog is truly THE BEST BOOK CATALOG IN THE WORLD! Order yours today — you will be very pleased, we know.*

**LOOMPANICS UNLIMITED
PO BOX 1197
PORT TOWNSEND, WA 98368
USA**